CONTENTS

What's inside...

07 WELCOME
Mike Wild introduces the 2023 *Hornby Magazine* Yearbook while reflecting on the big events of the past year.

08 REVIEW OF THE YEAR 2021-2022
It has been another incredibly busy twelve months for model railway manufacturers with plenty of new models arriving at retailers to tempt modellers. Mark Chivers looks back at the year's major releases.

18 MODELLING THE BIG FOUR
The centenary of the Grouping in 1923 is the perfect opportunity to model this fascinating period. Mike Wild explores what you need to recreate the 1923-1947 era in 'OO' gauge using readily available locomotives and rolling stock.

26 GETTING TO GRIPS WITH GARRATTS
Tim Shackleton reviews the fleet, noting how his weathering techniques have evolved in recent years.

34 DIESEL DEPOT INSPIRATION
A diesel depot makes a great standalone model railway or can be part of a larger scene. Ian Goodman highlights a group of inspirational depot scenes in 'OO', 'N' and 'O' gauge.

42 REALITY CHECK – THE 1923 GROUPING, 100 YEARS ON
While Britain's railway system was built in an era of optimism, it soon became apparent that the opposite was the case. As a result, the Government had to intervene to avoid catastrophic financial failure in 1923. Evan Green-Hughes explains the formation of the 'Big Four'.

52 LOCOMAN SOUND FOR THE HORNBY '9F'
The arrival of Hornby's all-new and stunning model of the BR '9F' 2-10-0 provided a sound installation project too good to resist. Mike Wild shows how you can install sound into the Hornby '9F' as designed and with optional extras.

58 MASTERPIECES IN THE GALLERY
We present a selection of the best layouts and model photography from the past 12 months in *Hornby Magazine*.

70 SWITHLAND VIADUCT
The missing piece of the *Hornby Magazine* Great Central Railway layout is finally complete: Swithland Reservoir bridge. Mike Wild explains how Paul Chapman's superb scratchbuilt viaduct was installed into the layout.

78 SUPER-DETAILED NORTH EASTERN WORKHORSE
Even modelling examples of ubiquitous steam locomotive types can present unique challenges for detailing, as Richard Hall demonstrates by comprehensively reworking Oxford Rail's J27 into 65894 as currently preserved.

86 TOOLS FOR THE JOB
Using a *Hornby Magazine*/Dapol Stove R model as a demonstration piece, Tim Shackleton takes advantage of years of experience to show how the right tools make kit-building so much easier.

92 DIESEL DEPOT DAWN

While the story of the development of British Railways' fleet of early diesels is often written about, less well known is the detail of how maintenance staff coped with this new form of traction. Evan Green-Hughes looks at the changes made to depots and servicing facilities in the early modernisation era.

100 BIOMASS FOR THE MASSES

2022 saw the arrival of Accurascale's most modern 'Powering Britain' collection freight wagons – the HYA and IIA fleet. Mike Wild models the latest power station trains by weathering a Hornby GBRf Class 60 and a rake of Accurascale IIA biomass bogie hoppers for 'OO' gauge.

108 'TT:120' IS HERE!

For the first time in 50 years a new model railway scale has come to the British market. Mike Wild details the launch of 'TT:120' – a scale which is set to make a big splash in the world of model railways.

118 FORWARD TO 2023

Mike Wild surveys the new models planned for the year ahead and beyond for the major scales and gauges.

Who did it? KEY

ISBN 978 1 80282 552 7
Editor: Mike Wild
Assistant: Mark Nicholls
Senior editor, specials: Roger Mortimer
Email: roger.mortimer@keypublishing.com
Design: SJmagic DESIGN SERVICES, India
Cover: Dan Hilliard
Advertising Sales Manager: Brodie Baxter
Email: brodie.baxter@keypublishing.com
Tel: 01780 755131
Advertising Production: Debi McGowan
Email: debi.mcgowan@keypublishing.com

SUBSCRIPTION/MAIL ORDER

Key Publishing Ltd, PO Box 300, Stamford, Lincs, PE9 1NA
Tel: 01780 480404
Subscriptions email: subs@keypublishing.com
Mail Order email: orders@keypublishing.com
Website: www.keypublishing.com/shop

PUBLISHING

Group CEO: Adrian Cox
Publisher, Books and Bookazines: Jonathan Jackson
Head of Marketing: Shaun Binnington
Published by
Key Publishing Ltd, PO Box 100, Stamford, Lincs, PE9 1XQ
Tel: 01780 755131 Website: www.keypublishing.com

PRINTING

Precision Colour Printing Ltd, Haldane, Halesfield 1, Telford, Shropshire. TF7 4QQ

DISTRIBUTION

Seymour Distribution Ltd, 2 Poultry Avenue, London, EC1A 9PU
Enquiries Line: 02074 294000

Welcome

WELCOME TO THE 2023 *Hornby Magazine Yearbook* – and what a year it has been. New product announcements have come through thick and fast, and we have seen a stunning collection of new models arrive in the shops to feature in the review pages of *Hornby Magazine*. However, the big news in 2022 was the launch of 'TT:120' scale through Hornby and Peco.

'TT:120' is a halfway scale between the ever popular 'OO' gauge and the smallest mainstream British scale of 'N'. It is the first all-new scale to be launched in the UK for 50 years and is set to offer a new choice for building a model railway that meets the need to save space in modern homes while being bigger than 'N' gauge.

The idea of 'TT' (TableTop) modelling isn't new, as the 1960s saw Tri-ang create a short-lived range of 3mm scale models that ran on 12mm gauge track to 1:100 scale. 'TT:120's' stand out difference is that for the first time these models will have true scale track and locomotives from the start.

Hornby's launch of 'TT:120' came in October 2022 and by the time you read this Yearbook the first products should be just about to arrive in the shops. There is a long-term plan for releases, which you can read more about on pages 108-115, and you can be sure to keep up to date with the latest 'TT:120' information in the monthly editions of *Hornby Magazine*.

Another highlight of the year was construction of Pete Waterman's Making Tracks II layout for Chester Cathedral. This superb model of the West Coast Main Line also attended the Great Electric Train Show where Pete and the Railnuts team revealed they would be building Making Tracks III for summer 2023 in Chester Cathedral and a third visit to the Great Electric Train Show.

This annual Yearbook is full to the rafters with inspirational features from the *Hornby Magazine* modelling team, including a full sound installation guide for the new Hornby 'OO' gauge BR '9F' 2-10-0 using a new sound profile from Locoman Sounds, construction of the final piece of our GCR layout jigsaw, a modelling guide for biomass trains using Accurascale's 2022-released IIA bogie hoppers plus our annual Review of the Year for 2021-2022 and our Forward to 2023 survey looking ahead at what you can expect in the coming year.

As ever, the model railway hobby is busy and thriving with new products in development for ready-to-run across six different gauges, including the growing interest in narrow gauge modelling. In fact, so rapid has the narrow gauge pace been that Bachmann has revealed and released two narrow gauge locomotives since the last Yearbook in the form of the Ffestiniog Double Fairlie 0-4-4-0T and Penrhyn Hunslet main line 0-4-0STs.

From all the team at *Hornby Magazine*, we hope you enjoy the 15th edition of the Yearbook, and we look forward to seeing everyone at events across the country in 2023.

Happy modelling!

**Mike Wild
Publisher, Modelling**

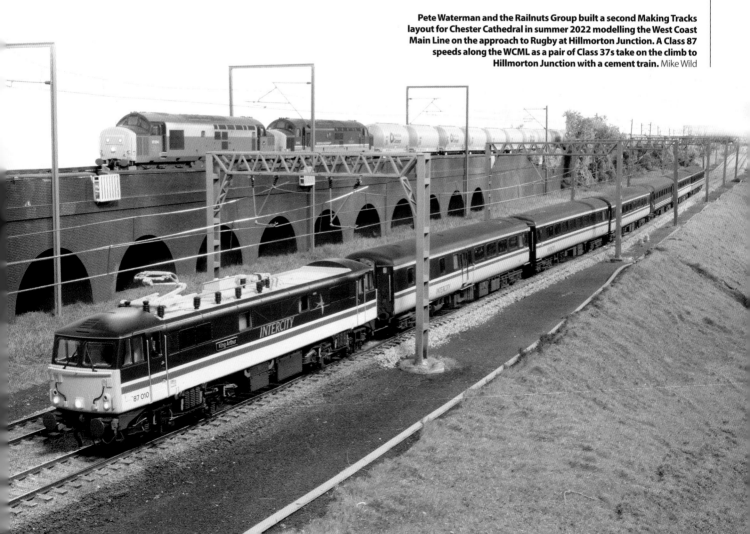

Pete Waterman and the Railnuts Group built a second Making Tracks layout for Chester Cathedral in summer 2022 modelling the West Coast Main Line on the approach to Rugby at Hillmorton Junction. A Class 87 speeds along the WCML as a pair of Class 37s take on the climb to Hillmorton Junction with a cement train. *Mike Wild*

Review of the Year
2021-2022

It has been another incredibly busy twelve months for model railway manufacturers with plenty of new models arriving at retailers to tempt modellers. **MARK CHIVERS** looks back at some of the year's major releases.

Despite the many challenges facing manufacturers over the past year, ranging from the lingering effects of the COVID Pandemic to soaring costs of raw materials and labour, 2022 has been another phenomenal period for new releases with almost 70 'OO', 'N', 'O' and 'OO9' completed model projects appearing – a marked increase over the past couple of years.

Certainly, the level of new announcements has continued at quite a pace with an impressive array of new models revealed as part of Hornby and Heljan's annual announcements, as well as the regular quarterly new model plans from Bachmann and ad-hoc announcements from the likes of Accurascale, Dapol, Rapido Trains UK, Revolution Trains and more across the year – more commonly coinciding with major model railway exhibition appearances. The year has also witnessed the launch of a new scale – 'TT:120' – with Peco and, most recently, Hornby revealing exciting plans for this new UK outline modelling scale – see more in Forward to 2023 on pages 118-127.

Looking at this year's new releases in more detail, of the new model projects that have been completed, 52 were 'OO', eight 'O', six 'N' and three 'OO9' gauge models. Delving deeper, of the 52 'OO' gauge projects, 22 were locomotives or multiple units, while six were carriage projects and, interestingly, 24 were wagons. In 'O' gauge, there were five new 'O' gauge locomotive projects completed, together with two wagons and one set of all-new 'O' gauge carriages. As for 'N' gauge projects, there were four new multiple unit models completed and two all-new wagons. Finally, for 'OO9' modellers, two stand-out all-new locomotives appeared, together with a set of four-wheel hopper wagons.

For the purposes of the survey, some projects have been grouped – such as Hattons' all-new 'OO' gauge Genesis four and six-wheel carriages, Hornby's new 'OO' gauge BR Mk 4s, Bachmann's all-new 'OO' Bulleid carriages, Accurascale's newly-tooled HAA merry-go-round wagons and the like. However, for clarity, some projects such as Revolution Trains' all-new 'N' gauge Class 320 and 321 Electric Multiple Units (EMUs) and Bachmann's Graham Farish Class 319 EMU and Class 769 Bi-Mode Multiple Unit have been included as separate projects, even though they may share tooling between them.

Bachmann completed 12 model projects during the past 12 months, while Accurascale delivered 11, Hornby 10, Heljan seven, Revolution Trains six, Dapol four, Oxford Rail three, Rapido Trains UK three, KR Models two, Ellis Clark Trains two, Peco two and the remainder one each.

In all, 33 locomotive projects, seven carriage projects and 29 wagon projects across all scales have been completed in the past 12 months, which when considered against the backdrop of economic and logistical issues is no mean feat at all – and there are plenty more in the pipeline to come.

Locomotives

So to this year's new releases in more detail, starting with Bachmann which completed

Hornby had a busy year in 2021-2022, with seven new locomotive models being released over the past 12-months. An undoubted highlight was the arrival of the Gresley 'W1' 4-6-4 in original 'Hush Hush' high-pressure boiler format. Here the lead grey 'Hudson' leads a Pullman train along the Topley Dale diversion route.

12 new projects – two of which were exclusive commissions for retailers.

One of the surprises for the year was an all-new 'OO' gauge Class 47, announced as part of Bachmann's Autumn 2021 quarterly model announcements. This latest version of the Class 47 arrived during October and was offered in three different variants – Digital Command Control (DCC) ready, DCC sound-fitted and DCC sound-fitted deluxe. The specification included all-wheel drive and pick-up, five-pole motor, twin flywheels and PluX22 DCC decoder socket. For this release, Bachmann introduced a new variation to the standard models with a sound-fitted deluxe model, which also included independently controlled roof fans and a special tint to the cab windscreen glazing, to reflect that seen on the prototypes.

For its next release, Bachmann worked with Locomotion Models and Rails of Sheffield to produce a 'OO' gauge model of the National Collection's London and North Western Railway's 'Improved Precedent' 2-4-0. As expected, this delightful model didn't disappoint and featured a coreless motor, 21-pin DCC decoder socket, factory-fitted 15mm x 11mm cube speaker, traction tyre fitted rear driving wheel and a representation of the inside Allan valve gear beneath the boiler.

In January, Bachmann's collaboration with Rails of Sheffield to produce a 'OO' gauge model of the Caledonian '812' 0-6-0 came to fruition, with five limited edition models completed for the retailer. They were offered in DCC ready and DCC sound-fitted formats, each model featuring a coreless motor, Next18 DCC decoder socket, firebox flicker, fully detailed cab

Rails of Sheffield and Heljan partnered to create a first-ever ready-to-run model of the GWR ordered, Swiss-built Brown Boveri gas turbine prototype 18000 for 'OO' gauge.

interior and representation of the inside motion below the boiler. Prototypical detail differences were also incorporated between releases.

Bachmann's recent trend of retooling some of its signature diesel models continued with the arrival of an all-new 'OO' gauge Class 20/0. This followed the introduction of the newly tooled 'OO' Class 20/3 Bo-Bo in 2021 (HM164). While almost a year had passed since the Class 20/3 had been released, the wait was worth it. Several Class 20/0 models had appeared later in 2021, with our review model of the Class 20/0 arriving during January. This latest addition featured a five-pole motor, PluX22 DCC decoder

socket, detailed cab interior, cab illumination and working directional lights – our sample featuring headcode discs with four headcode lamps and two red tail lights.

Completing the all-new 'OO' gauge releases, Bachmann also provided a surprise at the annual Diesel and Electric Modellers United (DEMU) showcase in Sutton Coldfield in July when it unveiled an all-new Class 37/4 Co-Co diesel. This was just one of a raft of all-new 'OO' Class 37

locos subsequently unveiled as part of its Autumn British Model Railway Announcement in early August. Our review model of the Class 37/4 was finished as 37401 *Mary Queen of Scots* in InterCity Mainline livery. Again, the model had been designed from scratch with a raft of prototype specific detailing incorporated within the extensive tooling suite – even the brake actuator chains have been modelled on the bogies. Three ❯❯

versions were offered for each model in DCC ready, DCC sound-fitted and DCC sound-fitted deluxe, with the latter examples featuring independently controlled roof fans and tinted glazing, in addition to the raft of lighting options incorporated.

Hornby delivered its newly tooled 'OO' gauge Gresley 'W1' 4-6-4 during December 2021, finished as 10000 in original lead grey. The model was announced as part of Hornby's 2020 catalogue range, with three models planned initially, together with an additional example added as part of Hornby's 2022 range. Hornby's initial release certainly captured the unique bulbous appearance of the prototype, coupled to its eight-wheel corridor tender. For those looking to model the later rebuilt version of the 'W1', the wait was a matter of months when Hornby issued the model in this later form during February. As with the original, the 'W1' featured

Freight stock was a regular part of the Accurascale collection in 2021-2022 including arrival of its BR 21ton mineral wagons in BR grey and bauxite liveries with detail differences.

Bachmann brought full attention to 'OO9' narrow gauge modelling with the announcement and immediate release of its 4mm scale model of the Ffestiniog Railway Double Fairlie 0-4-4-0T in November 2021. Here *David Lloyd George* pauses at Fairlie Syniad Da – *Hornby Magazine's* narrow gauge project layout inspired by the arrival of these models.

Peco completed its ready-to-run 'OO9' narrow gauge model of the Small England 0-4-0STT with Kato – the perfect partner to Bachmann's Double Fairlie.

a five-pole motor, brass flywheel and 8-pin DCC decode socket. Our review samples were finished as 10000 in LNER garter blue and 60700 in BR lined green with early crests.

February was also a memorable month in that Hornby also released its eagerly awaited 'OO' gauge model of BR's Advanced Passenger Train (APT). Two versions of the Class 370 APTs were produced with a five and seven-car train pack offered, in original and later style of livery applied. Extra articulated trailer car twin-vehicle add-on packs were also produced enabling train formations of up to 14 vehicles to be accurately created with Trailer Standard, Trailer First, Trailer Unclassified and Trailer Restaurant Buffet trailers produced. Hornby also accurately portrayed the different pantograph styles between the two train packs – one featuring a Faiveley pantograph while the later period model featured a Brecknell Willis »

TABLE 1 – 2021-2022 NEW READY-TO-RUN LOCOMOTIVES

Model	Scale	Manufacturer	Released	Featured
Brown Boveri gas turbine A1A-A1A	'OO'	Rails of Sheffield/Heljan	October 2021	HM174
BR Class 47 Co-Co	'OO'	Bachmann	October 2021	HM174
LNWR 'Improved Precedent' 2-4-0	'OO'	Locomotion/Rails/Bachmann	October 2021	HM174
BR Class 47 Co-Co	'O'	Heljan	October 2021	HM174
Ffestiniog Railway Double Fairlie 0-4-4-0T	'OO9'	Bachmann	November 2021	HM175
LSWR 'A12' 0-4-2	'OO'	OO Works	November 2021	HM175
BR Class 40 1Co-Co1 (new body tooling)	'O'	Heljan	November 2021	HM175
LNER 'W1' 4-6-4	'OO'	Hornby	December 2021	HM176
GWR 'Large Prairie' 2-6-2T	'OO'	Dapol	December 2021	HM176
Caledonian Railway '812' 0-6-0	'OO'	Rails of Sheffield/Bachmann	January 2022	HM177
BR Class 20/0 Bo-Bo (new tooling)	'OO'	Bachmann	January 2022	HM177
LNER rebuilt 'W1' 4-6-4	'OO'	Hornby	February 2022	HM178
BR Class 370 Advanced Passenger Train	'OO'	Hornby	February 2022	HM178
BR Class 86/4 Bo-Bo	'OO'	Heljan	February 2022	HM178
BR Class 14 0-6-0DH	'O'	Minerva Model Railways	February 2022	HM178
BR Class 320 Electric Multiple Unit	'N'	Revolution Trains	February 2022	
BR Class 321 Electric Multiple Unit	'N'	Revolution Trains	February 2022	
LNER 'A1/A3' 4-6-2 (new tooling)	'OO'	Hornby	March 2022	HM179
Sentinel 0-6-0DH	'OO'	Hornby	March 2022	HM179
BR Class 121 diesel railcar	'O'	Dapol	March 2022	HM179
BR Class 91 Bo-Bo	'OO'	Hornby	April 2022	HM180
BR Class 56 Co-Co	'O'	Heljan	April 2022	HM180
Ffestiniog Rly 'Small England' 0-4-0STT	'OO9'	Peco/Kato	April 2022	HM180
BR Class 55 'Deltic' Co-Co	'OO'	Accurascale	April 2022	HM180
LU 1938 tube stock (motorised)	'OO'	EFE Rail	May 2022	HM181
Class 319 four-car Electric Multiple Unit	'N'	Bachmann/Graham Farish	June 2022	
Class 769 four-car Bi-Mode Multiple Unit	'N'	Bachmann/Graham Farish	June 2022	HM182
NER petrol-electric Autocar	'OO'	Rails of Sheffield/Heljan	June 2022	HM182
Fell 2-D-2 diesel	'OO'	KR Models	August 2022	HM184
GWR 'Manor' 4-6-0	'OO'	Dapol	August 2022	HM184
BR Class 37/4 Co-Co	'OO'	Bachmann	September 2022	HM184
BR Class 45 1-Co-Co1	'OO'	Heljan	September 2022	HM185
BR Standard '9F' 2-10-0	'OO'	Hornby	September 2022	HM185

Cavalex Models delivered its new TEA bogie tankers for 'OO' gauge with a choice of pristine and weathered finishes.

example. The model also featured detailed fully illuminated interiors.

Next to appear from the Margate based manufacturer was its upgraded 'OO' model of the LNER 'A1/A3' 4-6-2, which included newly tooled components such as new driving wheel profile, die-cast running plate and firebox flicker. Our reviews models were finished as 2564 *Knight of the Thistle* in LNER lined green and 60103 *Flying Scotsman* in BR lined green with late crests. March also witnessed arrival of the company's newly tooled 'OO' gauge Rolls Royce Sentinel 0-6-0DH. While this was a natural development from the earlier 0-4-0DH model produced by Hornby, this all-new example of the Sentinel was designed from the ground up. Fitted with a six-pin DCC decoder socket, our review samples were supplied in Port of Bristol Authority and Stanton Ironworks colour schemes.

Modellers of the East Coast Main Line scene have long been waiting for a high-definition model of the sleek Class 91 Bo-Bo electrics. While Hornby had previously modelled the Class 91 and BR Mk 4 rolling stock, the models were showing their age, so an all-new version was announced in 2020. In April, the manufacturer delivered on its promise with the first examples of the newly tooled project arriving. Four models formed the initial releases, with our initial review sample finished as 91111 *For the Fallen* in distinctive Virgin branded First World War commemorative livery. The finish was outstanding and our review sample ran superbly on test, thanks to its powerful five-pole skew wound motor, twin flywheels, all-wheel drive and pick-ups, together with die-cast chassis block. Hornby's latest 'OO' Class 91 also featured a new 21-pin DCC decoder socket, which enabled the manufacturer to incorporate a choice of

lighting options to better reflect prototypical use.

Hornby's final high-profile model release during the period under review arrived during September, with the arrival of its newly tooled 'OO' gauge BR Standard '9F' 2-10-0. The '9F' has enjoyed a long association with Hornby having been in the range since the 1970s and undergone a series of revisions through the years. This though, was an all-new model developed from scratch with a raft of detail differences incorporated – including five different tenders. Our review samples included 92167 in BR black with late crests and BR1K tender, 92194 in BR black with late crests and BR1F tender and 92220 *Evening Star* in BR lined green with late crests and BR1G tender. BR1B and BR1C tenders have also been tooled for future releases.

Danish manufacturer Heljan also had a busy year with four new 'OO' gauge projects delivered, including two retailer exclusive commissions. First to arrive was the impressive Brown Boveri gas turbine A1A-A1A 18000, produced exclusively for Rails of Sheffield, in its eye-catching black and silver colour scheme. It featured a die-cast chassis, engine room lights, cab illumination, factory-fitted speaker, separately fitted handrails, five-pole motor, twin flywheels, directional lighting and 21-pin DCC decoder socket.

For its next 'OO' gauge release, the manufacturer reworked the Class 86/4 Bo-Bo electric, following on from the popular Class 86/0 released earlier in 2021 (HM167). This new version features an all-new body tooling – suited to Class 86/4 and 86/6 variants – with excellent bodies and neatly shaped Brecknell-Willis single arm pantograph. As with the 86/0 the model is fitted with a 21-pin DCC decoder socket, twin flywheels and five-pole motor, together with revised lighting functions to

enable tail lights to be switched separately at each end.

In June, Heljan delivered the North Eastern Railway petrol-electric Autocar for 'OO', developed exclusively for Rails of Sheffield. Three versions formed the initial releases, including 3170 in 1902-1923 NER red and cream, 3170 in 1923-1931 LNER brown and 3171 in 1904-1930 NER red and cream. This delightful model featured ornate clerestory windows with etched glazing panels, interior seat detailing and neatly moulded engine bay mouldings.

As this issue of the *Hornby Magazine Yearbook* closed for press, Heljan delivered its most recent 'OO' gauge release of the Class 45 1Co-Co1 diesel. Heljan's newly tooled models focus on the original split centre headcode examples as well as the Class 45/0s with later sealed

beam nose ends and the Class 45/1 Electric Train Heating (ETH) examples. These impressive new releases feature factory-fitted buffer beam detailing, decorated cab interiors, etched metal roof fan grille, cab interior illumination, directional lighting and more. A raft of releases form the initial batch, including standard and limited edition models for selected retailers.

Dapol added two Great Western Railway locos to its 'OO' gauge roster this year, with the release of the Collett '5101' and '61XX' 2-6-2Ts in December, followed later in 2022 with the Collett designed 'Manor' 4-6-0s. Dapol's 'Large Prairies' impressed with their five-pole skew-wound motor, flywheel, Next18 DCC decoder socket (on Dapol's signature slide-out PCB from the smokebox) and firebox flicker. Equally, the GWR 'Manor' was a definite improvement over previous models of the loco with sprung metal buffers, copper capped chimney, brass finish safety valve bonnet, whistle, full-relief coal space and inside motion represented.

Accurascale delivered its first 'OO' gauge ready-to-run loco during the year, with the arrival of its newly tooled 'OO' gauge Class 55 'Deltic' diesels. There were high expectations of the all-new model and we weren't disappointed. More than 20 different versions formed the initial releases with a combination of standard and limited-edition exclusives available from selected retailers. As we have come to expect, a mind-boggling array of era-specific details have been incorporated between the various models, according to the

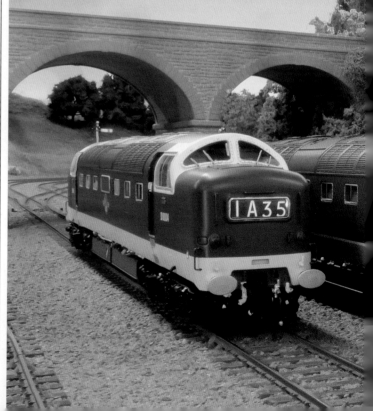

period each model represents, while access to the decoder socket was also simplified, thanks to a magnetic roof section that simply lifts off to reveal the decoder socket – saving the need to remove the bodyshell and the intricate brake actuator chains attached to the bogies and bodyshell. No surprise then, that it was awarded Best 'OO' gauge Locomotive in the *Hornby Magazine* Model Railway Awards during a ceremony at the 2022 Great Electric Train Show in October.

KR Models bolstered its portfolio with the release of the 'OO' gauge Fell 2-D-2 diesel loco. This austere looking model featured etched metal bonnet grilles and with fans behind, separately fitted handrails and lamp irons, turned metal spoke wheels, sprung buffers, factory-fitted 28mm diameter speaker and 21-pin DCC decoder socket.

Specialist manufacturer OO Works completed its 'OO' ready-to-run London and South Western Railway (LSWR) 'A12' 0-4-2 in late 2021. Our review sample weighed in at 400grams, courtesy of the model's all-metal construction, while combined with a high-torque coreless motor its tractive effort proved impressive – hauling a six coach rake of carriages with ease.

TABLE 2 – 2021-2022 NEW READY-TO-RUN CARRIAGES				
Model	**Scale**	**Manufacturer**	**Released**	**Featured**
SR Maunsell Dining Saloons	'OO'	Hornby	May 2022	HM181
LNER Thompson corridor carriages	'O'	Ellis Clark Trains/Darstaedt	May 2022	HM181
BR Mk 2f Driving Brake Second Open	'OO'	Bachmann	July 2022	HM183
BR Mk 4 carriages	'OO'	Hornby	July 2022	HM183
BR Mk 4 Driving Van Trailer	'OO'	Hornby	August 2022	HM184
SR Bulleid corridor carriages	'OO'	Bachmann	September 2022	HM185
'Genesis' four/six-wheel carriages	'OO'	Hattons	September 2022	HM185

Finally, for something a little different, EFE Rail delivered a motorised version of its 1:76 scale London Underground 1938 tube stock for 'OO'. It was to be two decades after its initial release as a static model that its full potential was realised, with motor bogies fitted to the Driving cars and interior illumination throughout.

'N' Gauge

It was a relatively quiet year for 'N' gauge modellers with Bachmann and Revolution Trains delivering two multiple units each. Revolution Trains' eagerly anticipated Class 320 and 321 Electric Multiple Units (EMUs) started to appear in late February with the first models released at the annual Model Rail Scotland exhibition in Glasgow – a limited edition of 320306 *Model Rail Scotland* in Strathclyde PTE carmine and cream. Subsequent models of the three-car Class 320 and four-car Class 321 EMUs were then released, including examples in Strathclyde PTE orange, ScotRail 'Saltire', Network SouthEast, London Midland and Silverlink colour schemes.

Bachmann also completed its long-awaited 'N' gauge Class 319 four-car EMU project during the year. First announced in 2016, models in Network SouthEast, Thameslink and Northern Rail colours were planned, while a version of the Class 769 Bi-Mode Multiple Unit (BMMU) was a more recent addition to the line-up. Our review model of the Class 769 featured detail differences incorporated such as the diesel generator sets fitted beneath each Driving Motor Standard (DMS) vehicle and ran smoothly throughout the speed range, powered by a coreless motor. Bachmann's Class 319/769 multiple units also won the *Hornby Magazine* Model Railway Award for Best 'N' gauge locomotive, even though it's a unit and not a loco.

'OO9' Gauge

Amongst its Winter British Model Railway Announcements, Bachmann revealed a newly tooled 'OO9' scale Ffestiniog Railway Double Fairlie 0-4-4-0T, which was not only a surprise, but it had already been produced and was in the country, with a review sample arriving in the *Hornby Magazine* office the next day! This stunning new model initially appeared in four variants and featured a coreless motor with drive to both bogies, all-wheel pick-up, factory-fitted 15mm x 11mm speaker and Next18 DCC decoder socket. Not only did the model look good and run well, it also spurred the *Hornby Magazine* team to build a brand new 'OO9' exhibition layout specifically to showcase the new model in action – subsequently named *Fairlie Syniad Da* (HM175/176), which translates as *Fairlie Good Idea*… Again, it was perhaps no surprise that »

Diesel era modellers were treated to the long-awaited arrival of the Accurascale 'Deltic' for 'OO' gauge, and this striking feature rich locomotive went on to win the *Hornby Magazine* Model Railway Awards Best 'OO' gauge Locomotive category. A trio of distinctly different Accurascale 'Deltics' line up on Topley Dale.

Bachmann's Double Fairlie was voted Best 'OO9' Locomotive, in the *Hornby Magazine* Model Railway Awards 2022

Peco also delivered on its 'OO9' promise during the year with the release of the Ffestiniog Railway 'Small England' 0-4-0STT, a collaboration with Japanese manufacturer Kato. This diminutive model featured a powerful coreless motor, traction tyres on the rear pair of driving wheels and pick-ups to all other axles. While the models released as *Prince* and *Princess* didn't feature provision for DCC, a digital sound-fitting guide was included in HM186 for those wishing to add this to their models.

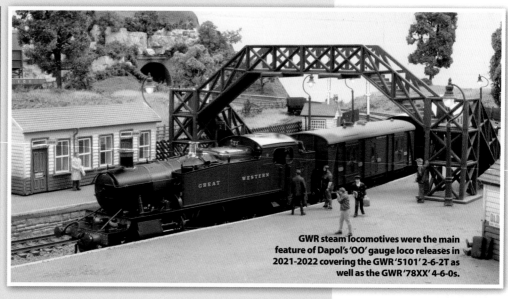

GWR steam locomotives were the main feature of Dapol's 'OO' gauge loco releases in 2021-2022 covering the GWR '5101' 2-6-2T as well as the GWR '78XX' 4-6-0s.

'O' Gauge

Five new 'O' gauge diesel models appeared during the year with three from Heljan and one each from Dapol and Minerva Model Railways. Heljan delivered its new 'O' gauge Class 47 Co-Co during October 2021, which features two all-new body shells to enable the manufacturer to offer a wide range of prototypical colour schemes. One is in original condition with headcodes, while the later example features plated headcodes and high-intensity headlights. At just over 3kg, this was a weighty model and featured a centrally mounted five-pole motor with twin flywheels, Cardan shafts to bogie gearboxes, powered roof fans, decorated and illuminated cab interiors and directional lighting.

Hot-on-the-heels of the Class 47, Heljan also delivered its new version of the 'O' gauge Class 40 1Co-Co1 the following month. This latest release featured new body tooling, representing the class in their final form with centre headcodes. Four unnumbered models were produced initially in BR plain green, BR green with small yellow warning panels, BR green with full yellow ends and BR blue with full yellow ends, together with a fully-finished model as 40155 in BR blue with full yellow ends.

For its third release, Heljan completed its eagerly awaited Class 56 Co-Co in April – which was subsequently awarded Best 'O' gauge Locomotive in the *Hornby Magazine* Model Railway Awards. The models were worth the wait, with Heljan's all-new releases representing the later Doncaster and Crewe built examples (56061-56135). It featured two powerful five-pole motors with brass flywheels, all-wheel pick-up, working roof fans, directional and cab lighting, space for a large scale DCC decoder and choice of flat or round profile handrails.

Dapol followed up its 'O' gauge Class 122 diesel railcar with the Pressed Steel Class 121 variant during March. Our review sample was finished in BR lined green with small yellow warning panels, while versions in BR green with 'speed whiskers', BR blue, BR blue and grey and GW150 chocolate and cream have also been produced. The specification includes a diecast chassis, bogie mounted motors, 21-pin DCC decoder socket, detailed interior, independent lighting and space for up to three speaker installations.

Finally for 'O' gauge, Minerva Model Railways completed its Class 14 0-6-0DH project during the year. It was offered unnumbered in BR two-tone green with DCC ready, DCC fitted and DCC sound-fitted options. Our review sample featured a five-pole motor, PluX22 DCC decoder socket and was supplied with optional loco transfer sheets for the numbers, etched metal builder plates and printed headcodes.

Carriages

Six all-new 'OO' gauge carriage projects came to fruition during the past twelve months, with Hornby's all-new Maunsell Dining Saloons arriving in May. These delightful new models were produced to complement the existing range of Maunsell models in the manufacturers range, particularly the First Class Dining Car. Two versions were produced as an Open Third in Southern Railway olive green and a Composite in BR Southern Region green. Bearing the hallmarks of the manufacturer's previously released

Hornby's latest release in our survey was its all-new BR '9F' 2-10-0 for 'OO' gauge, which includes a version finished as last-built BR steam locomotive 92220 *Evening Star* in BR lined green. The 2-10-0 rounds the curve from Quorn Magna on the *Hornby Magazine* test track.

Maunsell models, both featured detailed interiors, while the Composite also featured printed window glazing at the appropriate end. They were also the first of Hornby's new 'OO' gauge releases to include its new magnetic close couplings. Hornby's all-new Maunsell Dining Saloons were also voted winner of *Hornby Magazine* Model Railway Award for Best 'OO' gauge Carriage or Wagon.

Hornby also completed its BR Mk 4 carriage and associated Driving Van Trailer projects this year too, with a vast array of vehicles released in InterCity, GNER, LNER and Transport for Wales colour schemes. For the BR Mk 4 carriages, Hornby developed each of the varied vehicle types that make up full authentic rakes and also considered how the formations changed over time. As a result, the vehicles produced include Trailer Standard Open – End, Trailer Standard Open, Trailer Standard Open Accessible, Trailer Buffet/Restaurant First (pre Mallard refurbishment), Trailer Standard Buffet/Kitchen (post Mallard refurbishment), Trailer First Open and Trailer First Open Accessible variants. Even the Mk 4 Driving Van Trailers feature detail differences according to the period modelled.

Bachmann delivered a revised version of its 'OO' gauge BR MK 2f Driving Brake Standard Open (DBSO) in revised form following removal of the corridor connectors at the cab end of the vehicles. This was carried out for use on InterCity services by Anglia between London and Norwich, with vehicles produced in InterCity, Anglia turquoise, Network Rail yellow and Direct Rail Services blue (Bachmann Collectors Club exclusive).

Bachmann's all-new 'OO' gauge Southern Railway Bulleid carriages arrived with retailers in the final quarter of 2022, following a long period of development. Vehicles include a Semi Open Brake

KR Models second powered locomotive was the unique Fell 2-D-2 diesel for 'OO' gauge.

Third, Corridor Composite, Brake Composite and Corridor Third, with detail variations incorporated such as original 10in or later 15in window ventilators, as-built bodysides or later reinforcing strips, battery box and dynamo variations, guard's handrail styles and more.

Finally, Hattons Model Railways also completed its 'OO' gauge 'Genesis' four and six-wheel carriage project with the first batch of vehicles arriving during September. Seven different body styles have been tooled, while options for gas lights, oil lights and electric lighting have also been incorporated. Look closer and you will also notice underframe variations and differences to the wheels and roof between models. A new interior lighting system has also been designed utilising plunger style electrical connections at each corner, linked to pick-ups from the wheels.

Further developments

Meanwhile, for 'O' gauge, Ellis Clark Trains delivered a set of magnificent LNER Thompson

corridor carriages, including Third Corridor, Brake Third Corridor, Brake Composite Corridor, First Corridor, Restaurant First, Third Open, Gangway Brake, First Open and Restaurant Third Open vehicles. Colour schemes offered include LNER 'faux' teak and BR carmine and cream as well as a full set of 'Elizabethan' vehicles, also in BR carmine and cream. Each coach featured a die-cast chassis, etched brass sides, injection moulded roofs, separately fitted brass handrails, sprung buffers and magnetic rubber gangways.

Wagons

Of the 29 wagon projects completed this year, 11 of them are Accurascale 'OO' gauge examples. Leading the charge this year were newly tooled Diagram 1/107 and 1/120 BR 21ton mineral wagons in BR grey (unbraked) and BR bauxite (vacuum braked), reflecting prototypical differences between them and plenty of exquisite detail, especially underneath. In a related move, the manufacturer also delivered a selection of Coil A steel wagons, which

utilise the same underframe. Each featured a moulded light blue hood, which covered some impressive interior detailing including an 18ft long coil well and adjustable hood supports.

Next from Accurascale, were some altogether more modern wagons in the 'OO' HYA/IIA bogie coal and biomass hopper wagons. While the coal wagons featured full depth hopper bays, the biomass examples included the bay door and mechanism details (which keep the biomass payload dry during transportation), as well as subtle differences to the end panel ribs too. The manufacturer also completed its 'cut-down' HYA wagons too, which were converted for use on aggregates workings – some even retained the weld lines and remnants of the former GBRF lettering on the bodysides.

Staying with the coal theme, the initial batches of Accurascale's 'OO' gauge HOP AB and HAA merry-go-round coal hoppers started to appear in the first half of the year, with a selection of hopper wagons in BR freight brown, BR Railfreight red and EWS maroon. »

The BR Advanced Passenger Train made a splash with Hornby in April 2022 with a choice of early and late liveries as well as a full set of coaches to replicate a 14-coach formation.

TABLE 3 – 2021-2022 NEW READY-TO-RUN WAGONS				
Model	Scale	Manufacturer	Released	Featured
BR 21ton mineral wagon	'OO'	Accurascale	October 2021	HM174
BR 21ton Coil A steel wagon	'OO'	Accurascale	October 2021	HM174
HYA/IIA bogie coal/biomass hoppers	'OO'	Accurascale	January 2022	HM177
HYA 'cut down' aggregate hopper wagons	'OO'	Accurascale	January 2022	HM177
BR 12ton 'Vanwide'/VEA vans	'O'	Dapol	January 2022	HM177
IWA bogie holdall vans	'OO'	Revolution Trains	January 2022	HM177
BR 12ton 'Vanwide'/VEA vans	'OO'	Bachmann	February 2022	HM178
IWA bogie timber carriers	'OO'	Revolution Trains	March 2022	HM179
IWA bogie holdall vans	'N'	Revolution Trains	March 2022	HM179
IWA bogie timber carriers	'N'	Revolution Trains	March 2022	HM179
HAA merry-go-round hopper wagons	'OO'	Accurascale	March 2022	HM179
BR 20ton 'Pilchard' bogie open wagons	'OO'	Oxford Rail	March 2022	HM179
Great Eastern 10ton covered vans	'OO'	Oxford Rail	March 2022	HM179
Great Eastern 10ton banana vans	'OO'	Oxford Rail	March 2022	
RCH Gunpowder vans	'OO'	Rapido Trains UK	March 2022	HM179
SECR five-plank open wagons	'OO'	Rapido Trains UK	April 2022	HM180
SECR seven-plank open wagons	'OO'	Rapido Trains UK	April 2022	HM180
Consett 56ton iron ore bogie hopper wagon	'OO'	KR Models	April 2022	HM180
BR 20ton Presflo cement hoppers	'O'	Ellis Clark Trains	May 2022	HM181
102tonne TEA bogie tank wagons	'OO'	Cavalex Models	June 2022	HM182
Snailbeach four-wheel hopper wagons	'OO9'	Peco	July 2022	HM183
BR 50ton 'Salmon' bogie flat wagon (rev)	'OO'	Flangeway	July 2022	HM183
CDA china clay hopper wagons	'OO'	Accurascale	August 2022	HM184
SECR 'Dance Hall' brake van	'OO'	Bachmann	August 2022	HM184
NER Chaldron coal wagons	'OO'	Accurascale	September 2022	HM185
PFA 'Dragon' nuclear container (new tool)	'OO'	Accurascale	September 2022	HM185
PFA 'Novapack' nuclear container (new)	'OO'	Accurascale	September 2022	HM185
PFA 'Nupak' nuclear container (new tool)	'OO'	Accurascale	September 2022	HM185
PFA LLNW/2896 containers (new tool)	'OO'	Accurascale	September 2022	HM185

The HYA and IIA hopper wagon family covering original coal and later biomass and cut-down aggregate hoppers added further modern wagon choices for 'OO' gauge from Accurascale.

Some were offered in original condition, while others represent the vehicles in later life, with detail differences incorporated and appropriate data panels too. HAA, HBA, HCA, HAD and HMA variants are among the models tooled, together with the somewhat different CDA variant used for china clay workings in the West Country. Examples of these in EWS and DB branded liveries also appeared.

Turning the clock back almost to the beginning, Accurascale also delivered its Chaldron four-wheel hopper wagons during the year. These delightful and diminutive models featured fine magnetic chain couplings and really captured the essence of the pioneering railway wagons, while also adding another prototype to the company's powering Britain range. Indeed, the company's decision to model vehicles that have powered Britain also extended to a series of new PFA wagon packs, which feature newly-tooled loads including the distinctive Dragon nuclear container, more modern Nupak and Novapack nuclear containers and a selection of Low Level Nuclear Waste/2896 20ft ISO containers. Who knew there were so many different varieties of nuclear containers?

Bachmann's newly tooled 'OO' gauge projects included the long-awaited BR 12ton/VEA box van in a raft of colour schemes together with South Eastern and Chatham Railway (SECR) 'Dance Hall' brake vans, which spanned eras from introduction to departmental use in the 1970s and 1980s.

Revolution Trains plugged another 'OO' gauge gap with the release of its IWA bogie holdall vans and the later timber carrier conversions. They were supplied in twin wagon packs, with unique running numbers and impressive printed detail, together with many separately fitted detail parts.

In March, Oxford Rail managed to complete some of its outstanding projects with the release of the 'Pilchard' engineers' bogie ballast/sleeper wagon, providing a new departmental option for modellers of 'OO' gauge civil engineers trains, while the manufacturer's 'OO' Great Eastern 12ton box and banana vans also came to fruition.

Rapido Trains UK's wagon development also continued apace this year with further new projects appearing including the RCH Gunpowder Vans (GPV) and SECR five and seven-plank open wagons. The manufacturer has modelled three versions of the GPV, with ten models released initially in a selection of colour schemes, while it also delivered two five-plank and one seven plank open wagon as part of the latter projects, with these appearing in a selection of SECR, SR, BR and departmental guises.

Of the remaining 'OO' gauge wagon releases this year, KR Models also delivered its 56ton Consett Iron Ore bogie hopper

The BR HAA 32.5ton coal hopper was a highlight wagon release from Accurascale modelling the fleet through its lifetime.

wagons as triple wagon packs in loaded or unloaded form. Cavalex Models completed its 102tonne TEA bogie tank wagon project with an impressive line-up of models issued in pristine and weathered forms – the latter models really standing out amongst the crowd with some of the best weathering techniques applied to date on a model. Finally, Flangeway delivered its revised 50ton 'Salmon' bogie flat wagon for 'OO' during the summer, following the unfortunate dimensional errors that were discovered with the original batch of models.

'O' gauge

Two new 'O' gauge wagon projects were completed during the period under review, starting with Dapol's 12ton 'Vanwide'/VEA box van which touched down in the New Year after almost a decade in development. Four Vanwide's and five VEA's formed the initial batch of releases ranging from BR bauxite to BR Railfreight Distribution grey with yellow ends.

The other arrival was Ellis Clark Trains' all-new 'O' gauge BR 20ton Presflo cement hopper wagons, which arrived to high acclaim during May. Bristling with detail, these all new models featured a die-cast chassis, injection moulded body, sprung axleboxes, free-rolling turned metal wheels, sprung buffers, various ladder styles and choice of single or twin reservoirs. Ellis Clark Train's new 'O' gauge BR 20ton Presflo was also voted Best 'O' gauge Carriage or Wagon in the *Hornby Magazine* Model Railway Awards 2022.

Hornby expanded its industrial range with the release of its Sentinel 0-6-0DH for 'OO' gauge.

Smaller scales

Completed 'N' gauge wagon projects were few and far between this year, with Revolution Trains' all-new IWA bogie holdall vans and timber carriers the main releases for the scale. These were well-received by modellers and appeared in twin wagon packs with two sets of holdall vans in Cargowaggon colours, two packs with Norsk Hydro branding and a pack of unbranded wagons. The timber carriers were also issued in twin wagon packs, with four different sets available in Touaz branded blue. The latter wagons were supplied with factory fitted large blue stanchions, while a set of smaller red examples were also included to supplement or replace those already fitted.

For 'OO9' scale modellers, Peco introduced its Snailbeach and District Railway four wheel hopper wagons in July. These super new additions also featured commendably thin mouldings – the hopper body measuring barely 1mm thick.

Overall

So, despite the many issues still resonating around the World following the COVID 19 pandemic, with logistics issues and labour shortages, plus the increasing costs associated with the economic climate, the model railway hobby appears to be in a robust and buoyant place right now – certainly if this past year's releases are taken as a guide. There are plenty more projects in the pipeline, with more to come no doubt in the coming weeks and months (see Forward to 2023 on pages 118-127). Innovation certainly appears to be high on the cards, with several manufacturers now actively building new features and added 'play value', if you like, into the models. This is a welcome development and while inevitably this comes at a price, it is interesting to note that more often than not the models that appear to sell out quicker currently are the top end versions with all the 'bells and whistles'. Exciting times. ■

East Coast Main Line electric era modellers saw the arrival of Hornby's brand-new model of the Class 91 Bo-Bo electrics. This new generation model puts its predecessor in the shade in both detail and performance. Here 91111 *For the Fallen* recreates the East Coast franchise on our electrified cement works layout – East (usually West) Coast Cement.

Modelling the 'BIG FOUR'

The centenary of the Grouping in 1923 is the perfect opportunity to model this fascinating period. **MIKE WILD** explores what you need to recreate the 1923-1947 era in 'OO' gauge using readily available locomotives and rolling stock.

Motive power development, intricate liveries and the quest for speed were signatures of the Grouping era on Britain's railways. Prior to 1923, there were more than 120 individual railway companies, with the grouping bringing all of those together to create the 'Big Four'.

The newly formed group of railway companies was formed of the Great Western Railway (GWR), Southern Railway (SR), London Midland & Scottish Railway (LMS) and London and North Eastern Railway (LNER) with Scotland's services split between the latter two.

This period in railway history saw great changes. The dawn of the Grouping was a time when steam locomotive development was at its zenith and the newly formed companies vied to build the most powerful steam locos, not just for the publicity, but to be able to haul heavier, more luxurious trains at higher speeds over long distances. It was also a time when the identity of a railway company was key to its marketing and stature and all four companies established colour schemes for locomotives, rolling stock, stations and even road vehicles.

Reality Check on pages 42-49 goes into detail about the Grouping process, but in this feature, we will keep our focus on the model railway options. This period has always been well catered for in ready-to-run form, but recent years have seen a much broader spectrum of locos and rolling stock come to the market to make it easier than ever before to build a model railway set in the 1923-1947 period with authentic locos and rolling stock.

If you are choosing this period for your project, you might already have a preference in terms of region, but a little research will show that choosing the right buildings and adding the right colour theme to your station will set the scene. Think about the road vehicles too, as 1920s-1940s cars and vans were very different to today's and road traffic would have been much lighter. Stations were often lit by oil or gas lights, though electric lights would be seen at larger facilities. You'll also need to consider the figures on your layout for a truly authentic feel and the stunning collection of 3D printed items from Modelu3D would be our first port of call to give station staff and passengers a period appearance. However, what really makes the difference is the choice of locos and rolling stock, which we will look at company by company.

Great Western

The Great Western Railway (GWR) ran from London to the west, with it express services stretching along Brunel's 'billiard table' from London Paddington to Bristol, South Wales, Devon and Cornwall, as well as reaching

Birmingham and beyond. The GWR had a diverse portfolio of railways which included four-track main lines from London, challenging and steeply graded freight routes in South Wales, the tortuous Devon Banks to reach holiday destinations in Cornwall and quaint country branch lines.

The GWR locomotive fleet is well catered for in 'OO' gauge and anyone modelling this railway will become familiar with the 'family' resemblance of its loco designs. The 1920s era loco scene was led by George Jackson Churchward, who was replaced by Charles Collett as Chief Mechanical Engineer to the GWR in 1922. However, Churchward's legacy lived on as rather than reinventing GWR loco design, Collett sought to improve and advance upon those firm foundations.

At the start of the Grouping there were still many 4-4-0s in service, including the double-framed 'City' 4-4-0s, but long-distance express traffic had been put in the hands of the two-cylinder 'Saint' and four-cylinder 'Star' 4-6-0s. Both of these Churchward designs would be succeeded in the early Grouping era with the

arrival of the Collett two-cylinder mixed traffic 'Hall' 4-6-0s in 1928 and arrival of the Collett four-cylinder 'Castle' express locos in 1923 – the last of which were completed in 1950 after nationalisation.

The 4-6-0 wheel arrangement was a common theme for the GWR, which made use of this chassis to take on the fast running of the Great Western Main Line as well as the stiff gradients of the Devon Banks, with a range of locos being completed for different purposes, including 'Grange' and 'Manor' in the smaller category and the 'King' as the largest express engine class to be built by the GWR.

All of these 4-6-0s are available ready-to-run for 'OO', with Hornby offering models of the 'Castle', 'King', 'Star', 'Grange' and 'Hall', while Bachmann produces models of the 'Hall' and later 'Modified Hall', Dapol produces the 'Manor' and in early 2023. Accurascale is due to release its first 'OO' gauge steam loco modelling the 'Manor'. There were also the Hawksworth 'Countys' which were introduced towards the end of the GWR era.

However, there is much more to choose from. Long-distance heavy freight can be hauled by

The LMS motive power department thrived following the arrival of Sir William Stanier in 1932. The pinnacle of his locomotive development were the 'Princess Coronation' 4-6-2s. Hornby's model of 6220 *Coronation* leads the 'Coronation Scot' through the diversion route on *Hornby Magazine's* **Topley Dale layout.** Mike Wild

USEFUL LINKS	
KeyModelWorld	*www.keymodelworld.com*
Modelu3D	*www.modelu3d.co.uk*
Hornby	*www.hornby.com*
Bachmann	*www.bachmann.co.uk*
Accurascale	*www.accurascale.com*
Dapol	*www.dapol.co.uk*
Heljan	*www.heljan.co.uk*
Oxford Rail	*www.oxford-rail.co.uk*
Rapido Trains UK	*www.rapidotrains.co.uk*
Locomotion Models	*www.locomotionmodels.com*

ABOVE: **Durston models the GWR in the 1940s and was built by Brian Woolwich. Here a 'Star' 4-6-0 4064** Reading Abbey **departs with an express while a pannier shunts in the goods yard.** Trevor Jones

BELOW: **Cliff Parson's Gresley Beat models the LNER in the London suburbs in 'OO' gauge in the 1930s. Overlooking the Georgian town houses the railway is busy with freight passing and locomotives on shed.** Trevor Jones

the '28XX'/'2884' 2-8-0 classes, while in South Wales the '42XX'/'5205' 2-8-0T and '72XX' 2-8-2Ts were also heavily used on coal and iron ore trains, all of which are modelled by Hornby. For something a little different Heljan has made a model of the '47XX' 2-8-0s – nicknamed 'Night Owls' as they were mainly used on overnight parcels traffic.

At the smaller end of the scale both Dapol and Hornby produce models of the GWR 'Large Prairie' 2-6-2Ts covering the '5101' and '61XX' fleets, while the 'Small Prairie' in both Churchward '45XX' and Collett '4575' formats is available from Bachmann.

No GWR layout would be complete without a pannier tank – a design synonymous with the company – and happily there are a number of choices including the '64XX' auto-fitted locos, the classic '57XX' and '8750' series 0-6-0PTs and even the final Hawksworth designed '94XX' 0-6-0PTs, all of which are produced by Bachmann. A full list of current and in development GWR steam locos is available in Table 1.

Adding to the loco roster is an increasing collection of passenger and freight stock. For passenger accommodation, choices include Hornby Collett 'Bow-end' corridor and non-corridor coaches, while for the very end of the Grouping period you could also include a rake

of Hawksworth coaches in GWR chocolate and cream. New choices for passenger stock including Dapol's Toplight Mainline and City coaches, which are in-development, while those looking for new GWR era parcels stock will be pleased to see Accurascale creating a new model of the Siphon G milk and parcels van. Both of these projects are expected to be available in 2023.

Freight stock was extensive on the GWR and included everything from private owner coal wagons as well as the company's own collection of box vans, opens, flat wagons and more. Some of the more unusual wagons are available as kits, while ready-to-run caters for the likes of the box vans, open wagons and well wagons. Also worth considering – and this goes across all of the 'Big Four' railway companies – goods wagons often moved across the network meaning that it would be quite possible to see a GWR loco with SR, LMS or LNER vehicles in a mixed goods formation.

Southern Railway

The Southern Railway had a more eclectic back story as the Grouping saw the South Eastern & Chatham, London & South Western and London Brighton & South Coast Railways as well as smaller concerns amalgamated to create the new company.

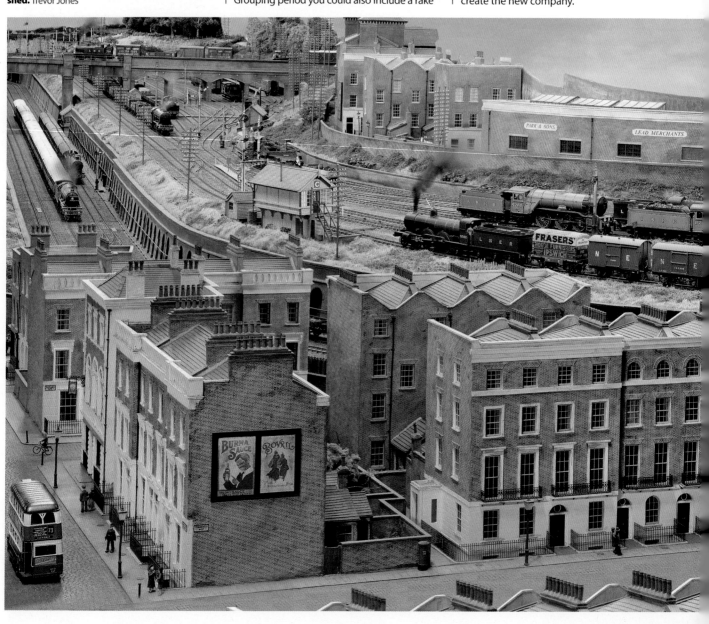

Murton Hall models a colliery setting on a branch line in the LNER era and was built by Dean Errington in 'OO' gauge. A Hornby Worsdell 'J15' 0-6-0 draws a set of coal hoppers away from the loading point while a Hatton's Andrew Barclay 0-4-0ST waits to shunt the next set of wagons. *Mike Wild*

TABLE 1 – GWR READY-TO-RUN LOCOMOTIVES 1923-1947		
Class	**Manufacturer**	**Status**
GWR '1361' 0-6-0ST	Heljan	Second-hand
GWR '1361' 0-6-0ST	Kernow Model Rail Centre	Second-hand
GWR '1366' 0-6-0PT	Heljan	Second-hand
GWR '14XX' 0-4-2T	Hattons	Second-hand
GWR '14XX' 0-4-2T	Hornby	Current (RailRoad)
GWR '1501' 0-6-0PT	Rapido Trains UK	In development
GWR '57XX'/'8750' 0-6-0PT	Bachmann	Current
GWR '64XX' 0-6-0PT	Bachmann	Current
GWR '94XX' 0-6-0PT	Bachmann	Current
GWR '56XX' 0-6-2T	Bachmann	Current
GWR '45XX'/'4575' 2-6-2T	Bachmann	Current
GWR '5101'/'61XX' 2-6-2T	Dapol	Current
GWR '5101'/'61XX' 2-6-2T	Hornby	Current
GWR '42XX'/'5205' 2-8-0T	Hornby	Current
GWR '72XX' 2-8-2T	Hornby	Current
GWR '2251' 0-6-0	Bachmann	Second-hand
GWR 'Dean Goods' 0-6-0	Oxford Rail	Second-hand
GWR '43XX' 2-6-0	Dapol	Current
GWR '28XX'/'2884' 2-8-0	Hornby	Second-hand
GWR '30XX' 2-8-0	Bachmann	Second-hand
GWR '47XX' 2-8-0	Heljan	Second-hand
GWR 'Dukedog' 4-4-0	Bachmann	Current
GWR 'City' 4-4-0	Bachmann	Current
GWR 'Castle' 4-6-0	Hornby	Current
GWR 'County' 4-6-0	Hornby	Current (RailRoad)
GWR 'Grange' 4-6-0	Hornby	Current
GWR 'Hall' 4-6-0	Hornby	Current
GWR 'Hall'/'Modified Hall' 4-6-0	Bachmann	Current
GWR 'King' Class 4-6-0	Hornby	Current
GWR 'Star' 4-6-0	Hornby	Second-hand
GWR Steam Railmotor	Kernow Model Rail Centre	In development
GWR AEC Railcar	Hornby	Second-hand
GWR AEC Railcar	Heljan	Current
GWR AEC Streamlined Railcar	Dapol	Current

This brought a broad church of motive power under the control of Chief Mechanical Engineer (CME) Richard Maunsell, ranging from Victorian era SECR locos such as the 'D' 4-4-0 and 'C' 0-6-0, to the more recent and powerful Urie 4-6-0s for the LSWR, which also included the 'King Arthur' 4-6-0s.

The Southern Railway ran out of London's Waterloo, Victoria, Charing Cross and London Bridge stations, with destinations including Dover, Brighton, Southampton and Weymouth. It also had a modest electrified network using a 750V DC third-rail power system, in use at 660V DC, as well as the Waterloo and City underground railway in London.

New motive power was soon introduced by Maunsell, with much of its taking direction from Urie's designs for the LSWR. Highlights included the 'S15' 4-6-0 freight locos, continuation of the 'N15' class 'King Arthurs', introduction of the most powerful 4-4-0 in the 'Schools' class and, for a short time, the most powerful steam loco on the British Railway network – the 'Lord Nelson' 4-6-0.

In 1937 Maunsell was replaced as CME by Oliver Bulleid who brought radical thinking to steam loco design with his air-smoothed 'Pacifics' as well as the characterful and austere 'Q1' 0-6-0s.

During the tenure of the two CMEs, the Southern Railway rapidly expanded electrification of the Southern Railway network with almost 300 route miles completed by the end of the 1920s.

The Southern was once less catered for in terms of ready-to-run models, but the past two decades have seen a big change and now an increasingly comprehensive collection of suitable locos is available off the shelf. This includes Bulleid air-smoothed 'Pacifics' in original condition, as well as the 'Q1' 0-6-0 from the same designer, while KR Models is currently working on a ready-to-run model of the famous, and short-lived, experimental Leader 0-6-0+0-6-0 steam loco, which never entered fleet service.

Locomotives of pre-grouping origin are also now widely available including the SECR 'C' 0-6-0, 'D' 4-4-0 and 'H' 0-4-4T plus the 'D1' is currently being developed in partnership between Rails of Sheffield and Dapol. Ex-LSWR classes include the Adams 'O2' 0-4-4T and '0298' 2-4-0WT that were originally made by Kernow Model Rail Centre and now reside in the EFE Rail range. Even the Adams '0415' 4-4-2Ts used on the Lyme Regis branch have now been made for 'OO' gauge.

Maunsell's designs are also well catered for with examples of the 'S15', 'King Arthur' and 'Lord Nelson' 4-6-0s all available from Hornby, together with the 'Schools' 4-4-0. Table 2 lists the full collection of 'OO' gauge Southern Railway locos.

Passenger rolling stock is now plentiful. Hornby has created an extensive range of Maunsell corridor stock as well as models of the ex-LSWR 58ft carriages and Bulleid 57ft corridor coaches, while Bachmann has recently released all-new models of the Bulleid 63ft main line corridor stock to join the SECR 'Birdcage' carriages.

Kernow and EFE Rail have released models of the LSWR 'Gatestock' push-pull trains and recently announced new book sets modelling ex-LSWR cross-country three-coach trains (HM187).

There is plenty of goods stock to choose from for the Southern Railway with Rapido Trains UK introducing a series of all-new SECR designed open wagons and box vans for 'OO' gauge with a choice of SR era liveries. In addition, there are ready-to-run wagons in the Bachmann collection including the classic Southern Railway ventilated van, while Accurascale has recently announced it will be making the Southern Railway banana vans introduced in the 1930s. Also recently released for 'OO' gauge as models of the LSWR Warner 24.5ton and SECR 20ton 'Dance Hall' brake vans from Hornby and Bachmann respectively.

London Midland & Scottish

Moving north of the capital, the London Midland & Scottish Railway ran out of London Euston and London St Pancras stations, with its network expanding north through the Midlands to Leicester, Birmingham and Nottingham to Manchester, Liverpool, North Wales, Cumbria and into western Scotland.

Its creation include bringing the London & North Western Railway (LNWR) and Midland Railways (MR) together, with the two companies having quite different motive power. The Midland had a 'small engine' policy, while the LNWR had much larger locos to rune on the

Cornwallis Yard models the Great Western Railway scene in the 1930s and features multi-level running with a shunting yard on the lower level and a through station on the upper level. Churchward 'Star' 4-6-0 4018 *Knight of the Grand Cross* passes with a down express for the docks terminus. On the right an '850' 0-6-0ST is the yard pilot today. Trevor Jones

West Coast Main Line on express passenger and heavy freight traffic. However, the LMS was still hampered by the 'small engine' policy in the early years of the grouping.

The creation of the LMS saw loco design in the hands of CME Henry Fowler who introduced bigger locos, including the 'Patriot' and 'Royal Scot' 4-6-0s as well as the impressive Beyer, Garratt 2-6-0+0-6-2 freight locos that were designed to remove the need for double-heading on heavy long-distance coal trains from the Midlands to London.

The big motive power changes came in 1932 when William Stanier took over as CME and brought his experience of working at the GWR's Swindon Works to the LMS. His successes included the 'Princess Royal' and 'Princess Coronation' class 'Pacifics', while his 'Black Five' 4-6-0 and '8F' 2-8-0 were also remarkable if less glamorous designs that lasted until the end of steam.

In 'OO' gauge LMS motive power is well catered for with examples of the main express locos – including the 'Patriot', 'Jubilee' and 'Royal Scot' 4-6-0s, plus 'Princess Royal' and 'Princess Coronation' 4-6-2s – all available ready-to-run, while the '8F' has been a long-standing part of the Hornby range too.

Currently in development by Hornby is an all-new model of the Stanier 'Black Five' as well as the unique 'Turbomotive' that used steam driven turbines instead of cylinders to drive the 'Pacific'.

This 1930s era Southern Railway branch by Colin Lockyer models a quayside terminus station in 'OO' gauge, with an Adams 'O2' 0-4-4T arriving with a single coach branch train. *Trevor Jones*

TABLE 2 – SR READY-TO-RUN LOCOMOTIVES 1923-1947		
Class	**Manufacturer**	**Status**
LSWR 'B4' 0-4-0T	Dapol	Current
LSWR '0298' 2-4-0WT	KMRC/EFE Rail	Current
LSWR 'O2' 0-4-4T	KMRC/EFE Rail	Current
LSWR 'M7' 0-4-4T	Hornby	Current
SECR 'H' 0-4-4T	Hornby	Current
LBSCR 'A1'/'A1X' 0-6-0T	Hornby	Current
LBSCR 'A1'/'A1X' 0-6-0T	Rails/Dapol	Current
SECR 'P' Class 0-6-0T	Hattons	Second-hand
SR 'USA' 0-6-0T	Bachmann	Current
LBSCR 'E1' 0-6-0T	Rapido Trains UK	In development
LBSCR 'E4' 0-6-2T	Bachmann	Current
LSWR '0415' 4-4-2T	Hornby	Second-hand
LSWR '0415' 4-4-2T	Oxford Rail	Second-hand
LSWR '700' 0-6-0	Hornby	Current
SR 'Q1' 0-6-0	Hornby	Second-hand
SECR 'C' 0-6-0	Bachmann	Second-hand
SR 'N' 2-6-0	Bachmann	Second-hand
LSWR 'T9' 4-4-0	Hornby	Second-hand
SECR 'D' 4-4-0	Rails/Dapol	Second-hand
SECR 'D1' 4-4-0	Rails/Dapol	In development
SR 'Schools' 4-4-0	Hornby	Current
LBSCR 'H1' and 'H2' 4-4-2	Bachmann	Current
SR 'King Arthur' 4-6-0	Hornby	Current
SR 'S15' 4-6-0	Hornby	Current
SR 'Lord Nelson' 4-6-0	Hornby	Current
SR air-smoothed 'BoB'/'West Country' 4-6-2	Hornby	Current
SR air-smoothed 'Merchant Navy' 4-6-2	Hornby	Current
SR Rebuilt 'Battle of Britain'/'West Country' 4-6-2	Hornby	Current
SR rebuilt 'Merchant Navy' 4-6-2	Hornby	Current
SR Bulleid 'Leader' 0-6-0+0-6-0	KR Models	In development
Class 401 2-BIL EMU	Hornby	Second-hand
Class 402 2-HAL EMU	Hornby	Second-hand
Class 403 5-BEL EMU	Hornby	Second-hand

Peaks 47 by Sam Jones models the final year of the LMS in the Peak District. A Fowler 'Jinty' 0-6-0T leads a branch train on the lower level while freights pass on the main line in the hands of a Fowler '2P' 4-4-0 and A Stanier 'Black Five' 4-6-0. Richard Watson

For the ultimate LMS era train, Hornby has produced models of the LMS 'Princess Coronation' in streamlined form as well as a full set of matching 'Coronation Scot' carriages allowing the stunning Caledonian blue and silver train to be replicated in full in 'OO' gauge.

Continuing the passenger theme, modellers can add rake of Stanier Period III 57ft corridor stock to their layouts as well as Stanier 57ft non-corridor coaches, both available from Hornby, while there are also plenty of freight wagons to choose from with LMS lettering, including a model of the LMS 12ton box van, open wagons and more.

London and North Eastern

Moving across the country the London and North Eastern Railway (LNER) had a broader territory than the LMS, which was also its greatest rival for Anglo-Scottish express trains. In fact the race to reach Scotland the quickest saw the LMS and LNER go head-to-head with streamlined trains as soon after the LNER had introduced its streamlined 'Coronation' service in 1935 on the East Coast Main Line (ECML) with the Gresley 'A4s'. The LMS added its own

TABLE 3 – LMS READY-TO-RUN LOCOMOTIVES 1923-1947		
Class	**Manufacturer**	**Status**
L&Y 'Pug' 0-4-0ST	Hornby	Current
Caledonian Railway 'Pug' 0-4-0ST	Hornby	Current
Midland Johnson '1P' 0-4-4T	Bachmann	Current
Midland Johnson '1F' 0-6-0T	Bachmann	Current
LMS Fowler 'Jinty' 0-6-0T	Bachmann	Current
LMS Fowler 'Jinty' 0-6-0T	Hornby	Current
LNWR Webb 'Coal Tank' 0-6-2T	Bachmann	Current
L&Y Aspinall '1008' 2-4-2T	Bachmann	Second-hand
LMS Ivatt '2MT' 2-6-2T	Bachmann	Current
LMS Fowler '4P' 2-6-4T	Hornby	Second-hand
LMS Stanier '4P' 2-6-4T	Hornby	Second-hand
LMS Fairburn '4MT' 2-6-4T	Bachmann	Current
Caledonian '812' 0-6-0	Rails/Bachmann	Current
Midland '3F' 0-6-0	Bachmann	Second-hand
Midland Fowler '4F' 0-6-0	Bachmann	Current
LMS Fowler '4F' 0-6-0	Hornby	Current
LMS Hughes-Fowler 'Crab' 2-6-0	Bachmann	Second-hand
LMS Stanier 2-6-0	Bachmann	Current
LMS Ivatt '2MT' 2-6-0	Bachmann	Second-hand
LMS Ivatt '4MT' 2-6-0	Bachmann	Second-hand
LMS Fowler '2P' 4-4-0	Hornby	Current
LMS Compound '4P' 4-4-0	Bachmann	Current
Highland Railway 'Jones Goods' 4-6-0	Rapido Trains UK	In development
LMS Stanier 'Black Five' 4-6-0	Hornby	In development
LMS Stanier 'Black Five' 4-6-0	Hornby (RailRoad)	Current
LMS Fowler 'Patriot' 4-6-0	Bachmann	Current
LMS Fowler 'Patriot' 4-6-0	Hornby (RailRoad)	Second-hand
LMS rebuilt 'Patriot' 4-6-0	Hornby	Current
LMS Stanier 'Jubilee' 4-6-0	Bachmann	Current
LMS rebuilt 'Royal Scot' 4-6-0	Hornby	Current
LMS Stanier 'Princess Royal' 4-6-2	Hornby	Current
LMS Stanier 'Princess Coronation' 4-6-2	Hornby	Current
LMS Stanier 'Tubomotive' 4-6-2	Hornby	In development
LNWR 'Super D' 0-8-0	Bachmann	Second-hand
LMS Stanier '8F' 2-8-0	Hornby	Current
LMS Beyer, Garratt 2-6-0+0-6-2	Heljan	Current
S&DJR Fowler '7F' 2-8-0	Bachmann	Second-hand
LMS diesels 10000/10001	Bachmann	Second-hand

A Billinton 'E4' 0-6-2T leads a three-coach Southern Railway branch line train through the fields on Colin Chisem's Hurst Green. This scene features a Bachmann Scenecraft oast house as well as a Bachmann 'E4' and Hornby Maunsell coaches. Mike Wild

with the streamlined 'Princess Coronation' class locos on the West Coast Main Line (WCML).

While the ECML was the spine of the LNER's territory, the company's reach also spread into East Anglia along the Great Eastern Main Line and into the Midlands with the Great Central Main Line, which gave the LNER a route to Manchester via the Woodhead route. Within this network of express routes the LNER also had a huge collection of secondary and branch line routes across East Anglia, Lincolnshire, Humberside, the North East and Eastern Scotland.

At the grouping, the LNER appointed Sir Nigel Gresley as the CME of the LNER and he led the companies locomotive and rolling stock policy through to early 1940s when Edward Thompson took over. Gresley's locos were highly regarded and included the 'A3' and streamlined 'A4' class 'Pacifics' as well as much more mundane designs such as the 'O2' 2-8-0 of Great Northern Railway vintage and the 'K3' 2-6-0. The LNER also inherited a large collection of pre-grouping designs including locos design by the Great Eastern, Great Central, North Eastern and North British railways.

In 'OO' gauge the LNER ready-to-run collection has expanded rapidly in recent years to offer a wide variety of motive power. Express engines range from the Ivatt 'C1' 4-4-2s through to the Gresley 'A3' and 'A4' as well as the Peppercorn 'A1' and 'A2' locos, while there will soon be an all-new model of the Gresley 'P2' 2-8-2, modelling the locos with and without streamlined smokeboxes. Perhaps most exciting for express motive power was the late 2021 arrival of the Gresley 'W1' 4-6-4 from Hornby in original and rebuilt forms, adding a unique piece of British engineering to the world of model railways.

Heavy freight locos include the Gresley 'O2' 2-8-0 together with the Robinson 'O4' 2-8-0 and Thompson 'O1' 2-8-0 from Heljan, Bachmann and Hornby respectively, while mixed traffic engines including the 'B1' 4-6-0, 'K3' 2-6-0 and 'V2' 2-6-2. Smaller freight locos on the LNER tended to be 0-6-0s and there are models of the GCR 'J11', GER 'J15' and NER 'J27' available off-the-shelf.

Passenger rolling stock is in good supply ready-to-run as Hornby produces models of the LNER Gresley corridor carriages as well as non-corridor 51ft Gresley and Thompson

compartment stock. Bachmann has introduced a new collection of Thompson corridor coaches with those suitable for the LNER era being the faux teak versions introduced in the mid-1940s.

LNER goods wagons are also available ready-to-run with example of 12ton box vans of LNER heritage available from Bachmann as well as NE branded open wagons, bolster wagons and more. Also worth considering are the recently introduced Accurascale Chaldron wagons that ran on internal railway networks in the North East coal fields through the grouping era.

Modern Marvels

Modern ready-to-run offers more opportunities to model the 1923-1947 grouping era with realistic locos and rolling stock than ever before, while present day printing techniques mean that the application of the intricate liveries painted onto locos and carriages in this era can be represented in full as well.

The colour of the 'Big Four' era makes this an attractive period to model and one which we can see being popular in 2023 as a celebration of this important turning point in the history of the British railway network.

TABLE 4 – LNER READY-TO-RUN LOCOMOTIVES 1923-1947		
Class	**Manufacturer**	**Status**
Peppercorn 'A1' 4-6-2	Bachmann	Current
Peppercorn 'A2' 4-6-2	Bachmann	Current
Thompson 'A2/2' 4-6-2	Hornby	Current
Thompson 'A2/3' 4-6-2	Hornby	Current
Gresley 'A3' 4-6-2	Hornby	Current
Gresley 'A4' 4-6-2	Hornby	Current
Gresley 'P2' 2-8-2	Hornby	In development
Robinson 'A5' 4-6-2T	Sonic Models	In development
Thompson 'B1' 4-6-0	Bachmann	Second-hand
Thompson 'B1' 4-6-0	Hornby	Current
Holden 'B12' 4-6-0	Hornby	Current
Gresley 'B17' 4-6-0	Hornby	Current
Ivatt 'C1' 4-4-2	Bachmann	Current
Bachmann 'D11' 4-4-0	Bachmann	Current
Gresley 'D16/3' 4-4-0	Hornby	Current
Worsdell 'G5' 0-4-4T (NER)	TMC/Bachmann	In development
Robinson 'J11' 0-6-0	Bachmann	Current
Worsdell 'J15' 0-6-0	Hornby	Current
Worsdell 'J26' 0-6-0 (NER)	Oxford Rail	In development
Worsdell 'J27' 0-6-0 (NER)	Oxford Rail	Current
Gresley 'J39' 0-6-0	Bachmann	Second-hand
Hornby 'J50' 0-6-0T	Hornby	Current
Holden 'J70' 0-6-0T	Rapido	Current
Worsdell 'J72' 0-6-0T (NER)	Bachmann	Current
Hunslet 'J94' 0-6-0ST	EFE Rail	Current
Peppercorn 'K1' 2-6-0	Hornby	Current
Gresley 'K3' 2-6-0	Bachmann	Second-hand
Thompson 'L1' 2-6-4T	Hornby	Second-hand
Gresley 'N2' 0-6-2T	Hornby	Current
Hill 'N7' 0-6-2T	Oxford Rail	Current
Thompson 'O1' 2-8-0	Hornby	Current
Gresley 'O2' 2-8-0	Heljan	Current
Robinson 'O4' 2-8-0	Bachmann	Current
Raven 'Q6' 0-8-0 (NER)	Hornby	Current
Gresley 'V1'/'V3' 2-6-2T	Bachmann	Current
Gresley 'V2' 2-6-2	Bachmann	Current
Gresley 'W1' 4-6-4	Hornby	Current
Sentinel 'Y3' 4wVBT	Dapol	Second-hand
Riddles 'WD' 2-8-0	Bachmann	Current

Getting to grips with GARRATTS

The LMS Beyer, Garratt 2-6-0+0-6-2s are amongst the biggest locomotives to run on the British Railway system. **TIM SHACKLETON** reviews his fleet of Garratts, noting how his weathering techniques have evolved in recent years.

People sometimes latch on to something I once wrote, said, or demonstrated as if it were as fixed and unchangeable as a legal statute. 'That's how you suggested we do it', they complain, 'but now you don't do it that way at all'.

The truth is, I've never been a great one for change and novelty – certainly not for its own sake – but even in my restricted biosphere fresh developments can and do happen. I'm also aware that, as far as weathering is concerned, there are many different ways of achieving similar effects and I'd like to think that, in trying most of them, I've built up quite a repertoire of techniques. In consequence the way I might do something changes not just year by year, but sometimes week by week.

Some technical aspects of model-making, however, are much the same nowadays as they were forty years ago. The refinement of detail of many of today's ready-to-run models is exceptional but take the lid off and the arrangement of such essential features as gear trains, wheel bearings, valve gear and current pick-up is largely unchanged. There's nothing remotely new about coreless motors – finescale modellers were routinely using them far back into the last century. We still assemble locomotive kits using flux and solder, we build plastic wagons using solvent adhesives, we wire our layouts – whether for analogue or digital control – in ways that would have been entirely familiar to a past generation of modellers. I've often heard it said that it's only the more artistic side of the hobby – in 'creative' areas such as scenic work and weathering – where change happens regularly and routinely, where new methods and materials arrive with almost monotonous regularity and disappear almost overnight. Dry brushing, anyone?

Individual preferences aside, there's no right way or wrong way to do anything, merely a range of alternatives. In this piece I want to look at how my approach to weathering has changed over time, and yet each method remains 100% valid today.

Everyone likes the ex-LMS Garratts so that's what we'll look at here, using as examples four Heljan models that I've worked on over the last few years. In some instances, the airbrush predominates, in others the emphasis is on colour washes or weathering powders. My preferred brands change along with the application methods, but there's no particular dogma attached to any approach other than the wish to bring models to life in the way that seemed most appropriate at the time. The consistent factor is the colour palette I employ – and that's exactly the same one I was using back in the days when BR steam ruled! ∎

Set among post-war housing estates on the western edge of Nottingham, Toton is a place I've visited many times over the years, but alas I was too late to see the Garratts, whose operational base this was. Modelling as a resource enables us not only to rekindle events from our memory banks but also to recreate scenes we never saw.

Even without the handy road sign, prior knowledge suggests the Garratt is on one of the branches serving the ironstone quarries just east of Wellingborough. Although single track, these railways were no bucolic branch lines but were heavily engineered on account of the heavy tonnage passing over them. The ore from the Northants field is iron-rich and that train of 40-odd fully loaded 27T tipplers would be hard work even for a loco like the Garratt. All images Jacy collection

My aunt sent me this postcard many years ago, and I've always treasured it. It shows 47974 hard at work on the Midland main line north of Elstree. Tim Shackleton Collection

Canklow shed, just outside Rotherham, was slightly off the beaten track for a Garratt but on 14 March 1953 47980 was in the process of dropping its fire prior to stabling. Jacy Collection

R.P 322

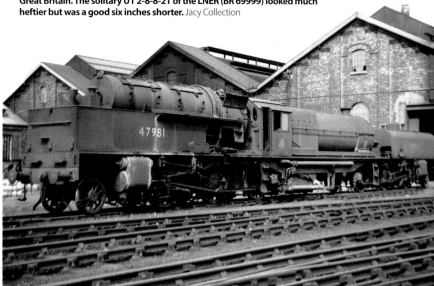

Looking exhausted, 47981 sits out the weekend at Toton in 1956. At just under 88ft the LMS Garratts were the longest locomotives ever to run in Great Britain. The solitary U1 2-8-8-2T of the LNER (BR 69999) looked much heftier but was a good six inches shorter. Jacy Collection

GARRATTS
fore and aft

47984 is going well as it powers through Wigston Magna in 1955. The engine looks virtually ex-works – like most heavy freight locomotives, I doubt if the Garratts were ever cleaned in service. Jacy Collection

STEP BY STEP **WEATHERING HELJAN GARRATTS FOR 'OO' GAUGE SKILL LEVEL: INTERMEDIATE**

1 On all Heljan Garratts, the numbers and BR emblems are over-scale, and need replacing with transfers. During the weathering process I'll be sloshing a lot of potentially malevolent solvents around and to avoid damaging the decals, I won't add them until quite late in the process.

2 Since the last time I weathered a Garratt, I've paid more attention to building up weathering effects in layers, beginning with an initial mist of grey-brown discoloration composed of a 50:50 mix of Tamiya Flat Black (XF2) and Leather Brown (XF64). This is sprayed thinly and unevenly, concentrating on the wheels and motion.

3 After adding more black to the mix, turning it into more of a dark grey, I've focused on the upper works. At one time I'd have used enamel paints for this, but nowadays I much prefer acrylics, not so much for their toughness as a base coat but because they dry so much more quickly.

4 The bunker and boiler top are sprayed with an even darker mix, which is simply another version of what has gone before. Remember that acrylic paints always dry lighter than they appear when wet. If you're unsure of the effect, test the colour first on something that doesn't matter.

5 The three different versions of the black-brown mix aren't so very different at all but give a subtle variation of tone that should be readily visible here.

6 This initial layer – more of a basic tinting than weathering as such – can now be left to dry overnight. Random streaks and dribbles add variety and should be encouraged as long as they don't sing out too loudly.

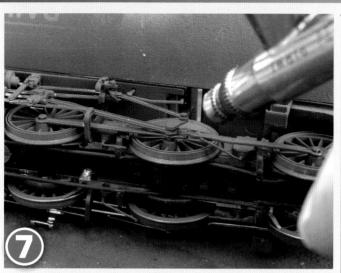

⑦

You'd need to put on an awful lot of paint in order to gum up the mechanism, but common sense suggests you should only use as much as is necessary to achieve the desired coverage. I'm spraying from less than an inch away at a pressure of about 20psi.

⑧

With the locomotive inverted in a foam cradle, I'm putting on a basic rust tone (Tamiya XF64 Red Brown again) that will underscore the final finish in the firebox area. The immediate visual effect, however, will come from weathering powders.

⑨

Once we've got to this stage I can put my airbrush down – for this kind of work I generally use an Iwata Revolution and notice how obsessively clean it is, inside and out.

⑩

Now we're going to be switching to hand-brushing using enamel washes. My preference for what's to follow is for flat acrylic brushes called shaders. These are from the ProArte Series 30 range and are very reasonably priced for a quality product. I haven't used expensive sables in decades.

⑪

Using my biggest flat brush, I slosh neat white spirit over the areas I'm going to be working on and immediately add little touches of MIG's Engine Grime, which is a warm darkish grey that to my eye perfectly captures one of the abiding colours of the working steam locomotive.

⑫

Around the bunker area I added quite an amount of Matt Black (Revell No 6 in this case) and brushed it well into the detail areas.

STEP BY STEP | **WEATHERING HELJAN GARRATTS FOR 'OO' GAUGE SKILL LEVEL: INTERMEDIATE**

13

The enamel wash is then worked in among the various surfaces of the model. If you miss anything at this stage, it probably doesn't matter because you've already got the initial discoloration from the acrylic layers. Any bald patches can be accommodated later.

14

Once the enamel washes have dried you can see the randomness that was the object of the exercise. This will later be knocked back as necessary with an airbrush. How very bright the fresh rust on the safety valves looks, though I used only tiny quantities of pigment to make the wash – we have to be careful not to be too strident in our choice of colours. Bland is good in this kind of context.

15

Now the numbers can go on. Waterslide transfers don't always like the enamel thinners used in weathering washes, so I've left them off until now. You can protect them with a thin mist of acrylic varnish or paint – LifeColor Burned Black (UA736) is my go-to shade for most retouching and blending-in.

16

The final embellishment is to add a selection of weathering powders. While other aspects of my approach may have changed, I've used the same core colours for a decade and more – I use such tiny quantities that one of these pots (now marketed by Abteilung 502) will last me for years.

17

The powders are brushed on and blended where necessary using flat, round-tipped brushes called filberts – this one is nearing the end of its useful life. Even for a thrifty Yorkshireman a bit of spillage is inevitable, but the surplus can be scooped up and reused.

18

I'm always sparing with my use of black powders. If I could make a comment about other people's weathering, it's that they often make steam locomotives appear much blacker than they actually were. Have they never heard of 'steam locomotive grey'?

19 An accumulation of coal crumb around the bunker really helps bring these models to life. Tiny detail touches like this can make all the difference, as long as you don't overdo things.

21 These two commissions arrived several months apart but what I hope you'll register is the consistency of my approach, as well as the subtle variations. When I do another Garratt, it will probably be different again.

20 I invariably photograph my models as they near completion and send copies to customers and friends inviting their comments. The Crewe-style repainted smokebox was much appreciated. I can see various steps that need straightening but otherwise I'm quite happy with it.

GARRATT COMPARE AND CONTRAST

Fixed-bunker Garratt from the June 2014 issue of *Hornby Magazine*, weathered using Humbrol enamels and MIG powders over a base coat of airbrushed LifeColor acrylics.

Here you see the importance of texture and surface finish suggested, in the smaller scales at least, largely by paint and powder – corrosion around the firebox, an oily sheen on the motionwork, coal dust on the bunker.

A rotary-bunker Garratt from my 2015 Ian Allan book, *Locomotive Weathering Projects*. Once again, we begin with LifeColor acrylics before switching to prepared washes from the Adam Wilder range. These days I prefer to mix my own.

There's a lot of detail weathering on this particular Garratt and most of it was achieved using powders. The variation of colour and tone isn't great but, built up in layers, it serves to bring the model to life.

Colour pictures of Garratts being mighty scarce, this private commission from 2022 drew heavily on my experience and ability to interpret material from monochrome sources.

We see a lot of our layouts from above, so we need to pay at least as much attention to the view from this angle as we do to things like the frames and motionwork. Whatever class of locomotive we're interested in, usable top-down reference photographs from any era are extraordinarily rare, so once again a lot of thought and insight is necessary.

Diesel Depot INSPIRATION

A diesel depot makes a great standalone model railway or can be part of a larger scene. **IAN GOODMAN** highlights a group of inspirational depot scenes in 'OO', 'N' and 'O' gauge.

Depots of any kind are fascinating places. Locomotives are at rest, some receiving maintenance and others stored out of use make access to these important railway facilities a wonderful opportunity. Naturally, the work carried out means access is restricted these days to keep the railway a safe place, but open days provide a chance to take a behind the scenes look at what goes into a depot.

Diesel depots began to form part of the railway infrastructure in the 1960s. The rapid introduction of new diesel locos meant they needed dedicated facilities away from the grit and grime of steam motive power to ensure that the new order was kept in full working order. Some depots were small parts of existing locations, where in others brand-new facilities were created like at Laira for the Western Region hydraulics. Other places converted steam

facilities to suit the new form of traction when the old order was despatched.

With the opportunity to display locos and add both detail and character, depot layouts have long been a popular choice for a model railway in its entirety, while other use the diesel depot as part of a larger scene including main line running.

In this feature we highlight eight of the best from the pages of *Hornby Magazine* to offer you ideas and inspiration for your own projects.

Lockton Lane is a 1980s era diesel depot built in 'O' gauge. Class 50 50011 *Centurion* ticks over alongside the scratchbuilt depot in the company of a pair of Class 08s. Mike Wild

1. Lockton Lane

Builder: Tim Lowe
Gauge: 'O' gauge
Period: 1980s

This busy 'O' gauge depot scene was built during the 2020 lockdowns by Tim Lowe to provide a perfect place in which he could both display and run his growing collection of 7mm scale diesel locos.

The main scene is compact at just 8ft x 2ft, but there is also an additional off-scene traverser storage yard that allows locos to arrive and depart from Lockton Lane. The track is all from the Peco stable using the code 124 bullhead range, while the main depot building is scratchbuilt around a plywood frame dressed in corrugated plasticard to create an authentic look. Outside the depot stop signs, barrels, bins, yard lamps and an overhead crane add to

the scene, while being a 1980s period layout there is also vegetation growing between the lines.

Fascinating is that the trackplan calls for just two points – one left and one right hand – but the addition of the off-scene storage yard makes for plenty of play value especially with the digital sound fitted locomotives which adorn Lockton Lane.

Lockton Lane originally featured in HM173.

»

LOCKTON LANE TRACK DIAGRAM (NOT TO SCALE)

10ft 6in

2ft

KEY

❶ Hardstanding	❹ Mess room	❼ Car park
❷ Gantry crane	❸ Depot	❽ Lineside hut
	❺ Fuelling point	❾ Railway overbridge
	❻ Low relief warehouses	❿ Traverser storage yard

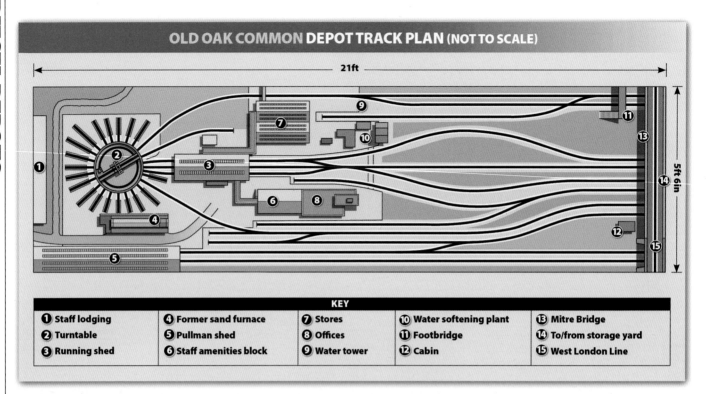

OLD OAK COMMON DEPOT TRACK PLAN (NOT TO SCALE)

21ft

5ft 6in

KEY				
❶ Staff lodging	❹ Former sand furnace	❼ Stores	❿ Water softening plant	⓭ Mitre Bridge
❷ Turntable	❺ Pullman shed	❽ Offices	⓫ Footbridge	⓮ To/from storage yard
❸ Running shed	❻ Staff amenities block	❾ Water tower	⓬ Cabin	⓯ West London Line

Old Oak Common was built by Malcolm Bentley to recreate his memories from the final years of the hydraulics on the Western Region. This depot scene is 21ft long!
Mike Wild

2. Old Oak Common

Builder: Malcolm Bentley
Gauge: 'OO' gauge
Period: 1970s

Of all the diesel depots to have featured in Hornby Magazine, Malcolm Bentley's stunning 21ft long model of Old Oak Common must rate as one of the best. It shows the true scale of a depot scene by modelling the famous turntable, running shed, Pullman shed and stores plus the stabling sidings on the approach to the depot.

Malcolm's layout was born out of a desire to recreate his memories of the late diesel-hydraulic era on the Western Region and features meticulously researched buildings and structures and an equally well researched collection of locos that includes a large number of 'Westerns' and 'Warships'. In addition, a visit to Old Oak includes 'Hymeks' plus diesel electrics of classes 31 and 47.

While turntables are generally seen as steam era features, the Old Oak Common turntable lasted into the 2000s and was an essential part of modelling this scene in the early 1970s.

Old Oak Common originally featured in HM186.

3. Oulton TMD

Builder: Allan Cromarty
Gauge: 'OO' gauge
Period: 1990s

The depot scene on Oulton TMD is part of a larger scene that also includes a station, cement and oil terminals as well as main line running. The main depot building can house up to nine locos and is fully detailed inside as well as featuring lighting. Outside there is ample stabling to accommodate the large 1990s era diesel fleet that runs on this exhibition layout.

Outside the depot is a pair of Knightwing fuelling points that are detailed

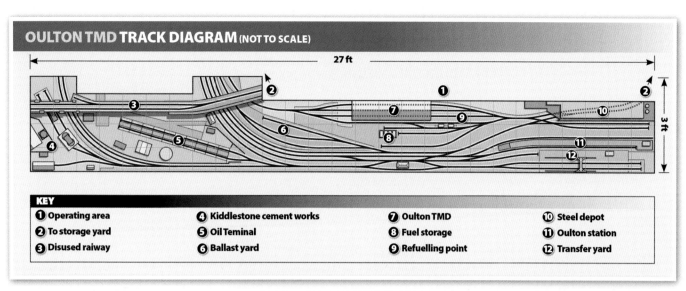

OULTON TMD TRACK DIAGRAM (NOT TO SCALE)

27 ft

3 ft

KEY

① Operating area	④ Kiddlestone cement works	⑦ Oulton TMD	⑩ Steel depot
② To storage yard	⑤ Oil Teminal	⑧ Fuel storage	⑪ Oulton station
③ Disused raiway	⑥ Ballast yard	⑨ Refuelling point	⑫ Transfer yard

with oil barrels and figures in hi-vis clothing to suit the period of the layout. Overlooking the depot yard are lighting towers. The trackplan in this part of the layout is relatively simple – long straight sidings which run through the external hard standing and depot building.

The 1990s setting of Oulton TMD brings a range of motive power including classes 08, 31, 37, 47, 56 and 60.

Oulton TMD originally featured in HM107. **»**

USEFUL LINKS	
Railway Laser Lines (buildings)	www.railwaylaserlines.co.uk
Modelu3D (3D printed figures and accessories)	www.modelu3d.co.uk
Scale Model Scenery (3D printed and laser cut accessories)	www.scalemodelscenery.co.uk
Bachmann Scenecraft (buildings and figures)	www.bachmann.co.uk
Gaugemaster (buildings and accessories)	www.gaugemaster.com
Skytrex (buildings and accessories)	www.skytrex.com
Sankey Scenics (depot signage)	www.sankeyscenics.co.uk

Roxby Town plays host to a large maintenance depot set in the modern era. It is based around the classic Peco depot buildings and built in 'N' gauge. Mike Wild

4. Seven Mill Depot

Builder: *Hornby Magazine*
Gauge: 'O' gauge
Period: 1960s

Hornby Magazine's diesel depot build took on the challenge of fitting a realistic 'O' gauge depot scene into 11ft x 3ft, including a storage yard.

The scenic area is 8ft x 3ft and features a fuelling point, two track depot building and space to house up to seven locos.

The scene makes the most of readily available products by using Skytrex castings for low relief buildings as the backdrop as well as the same manufacturer's kits for the fuelling point and storage tank, while the wooden fencing is a laser cut product from Scale Model Scenery.

The depot building is a Heljan plastic kit that has an interior benefiting from KS Laser Designs pits for added detail.

The period chosen was the 1960s suggesting a newly completed servicing point for diesel traction, but with a change of stock and road vehicles it could easily represent the 1970s, '80, '90s or 2000s era railway scene.

Seven Mill Depot originally featured in HM152.

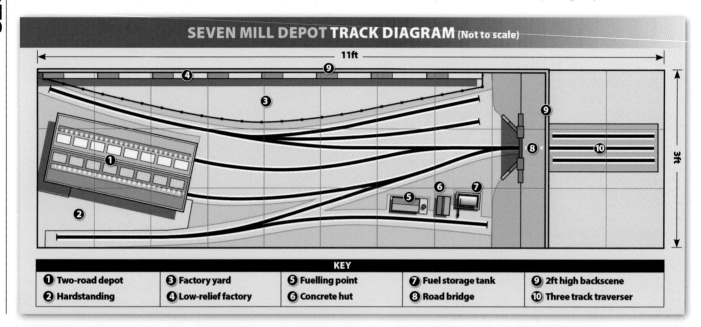

SEVEN MILL DEPOT TRACK DIAGRAM (Not to scale)

11ft

3ft

KEY

❶ Two-road depot	❸ Factory yard	❺ Fuelling point	❼ Fuel storage tank	❾ 2ft high backscene
❷ Hardstanding	❹ Low-relief factory	❻ Concrete hut	❽ Road bridge	❿ Three track traverser

Oulton TMD is part of a larger layout and provides servicing facilities for a fleet of 1990s era sectorisation locos. A trio of Class 47s are in attendance in this nighttime view. Trevor Jones

5. Roxby Town

Builder: Geoff Buttler
Gauge: 'N' gauge
Period: 2020s

Roxby Town is a layout of two levels – an upper level featuring main line running and a lower level that plays host to a bust depot scene. A link line on a gradient joins the two parts allowing locos and fuel trains to access the depot from the main line and return after servicing.

On the lower level the depot has a fuelling point, wash plant and a large covered depot over four-tracks that can host both locos and multiple units. The buildings are Peco diesel depot units, six in total, which have been joined together to create one large building.

This 'N' gauge layout models the present-day railway scene and is filled with bright contemporary liveries on classes 37, 47, 56, 57, 60, 66 and 67. Multiple units to be seen include the Class 220 and 221 Voyagers as well as classes 142, 156, 158 and 170.

Roxby Town originally featured in HM183. »

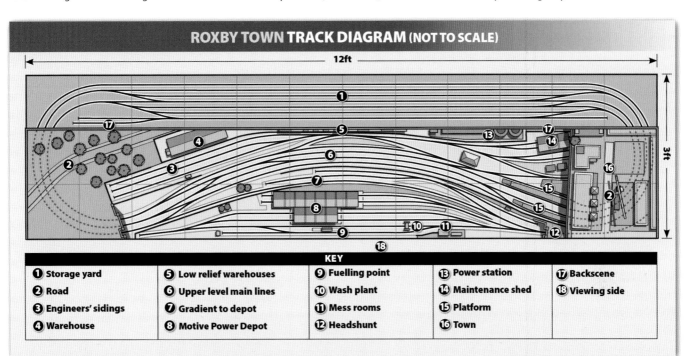

ROXBY TOWN **TRACK DIAGRAM** (NOT TO SCALE)

12ft

3ft

KEY

❶ Storage yard	❺ Low relief warehouses	❾ Fuelling point
❷ Road	❻ Upper level main lines	❿ Wash plant
❸ Engineers' sidings	❼ Gradient to depot	⓫ Mess rooms
❹ Warehouse	❽ Motive Power Depot	⓬ Headshunt

⓭ Power station	⓱ Backscene
⓮ Maintenance shed	⓲ Viewing side
⓯ Platform	
⓰ Town	

Barrow Hill Junction is a huge main line 'OO' gauge layout that also incorporates a large depot scene to house its collection of locos. With 23 locos on shed, there is still room for more.

6. Barrow Hill Junction

Builder: Michael Rhodes
Gauge: 'OO' gauge
Period: 1980s

This large 'OO' gauge layout includes a substantial depot alongside the station scene and provides a perfect place to host part of the loco fleet that has been assembled to run on Barrow Hill Junction.

The scene uses readily available buildings and structures from Bachmann's Scenecraft range, including the two-track depot, fuelling point, storage tanks and wash plant. Hard standing has been added around the base of the buildings with a second depot out of site to the left.

In total more than 25 locos can be accommodated in the depot, which includes two long stabling sidings alongside the main line.

Barrow Hill Junction originally featured in HM186.

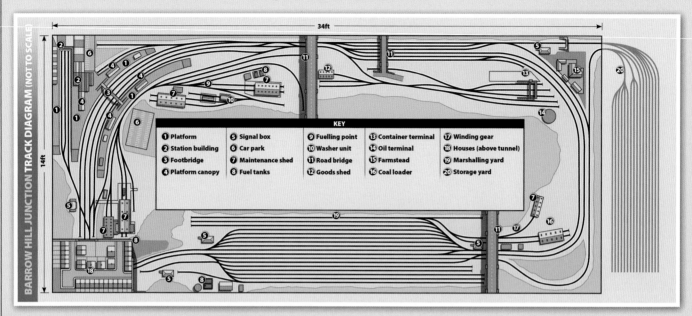

BARROW HILL JUNCTION TRACK DIAGRAM (NOT TO SCALE)

34ft

14ft

KEY

① Platform	⑤ Signal box	⑨ Fuelling point	⑬ Container terminal	⑰ Winding gear
② Station building	⑥ Car park	⑩ Washer unit	⑭ Oil terminal	⑱ Houses (above tunnel)
③ Footbridge	⑦ Maintenance shed	⑪ Road bridge	⑮ Farmstead	⑲ Marshalling yard
④ Platform canopy	⑧ Fuel tanks	⑫ Goods shed	⑯ Coal loader	⑳ Storage yard

In 2019 *Hornby Magazine* set out to build a compact 1960s era depot scene in 'O' gauge and Seven Mill Depot was the result. It uses readily available kits for the buildings and structures made by Heljan and Skytrex. Mike Wild

7. Talbot Lane

Builder: Marcus Lambert
Gauge: 'OO' gauge
Period: 2000s

Talbot Lane is one of the smaller layouts to feature here, but its modest track plan still offers plenty of potential for depot movements. The total footprint of the scenic section is 4ft x 1ft and uses the Bachmann Scenecraft single track depot building as its main focal point.

The building is illuminated inside and out, while yard lights also add to the scene to allow for nighttime running sessions adding more character to the layout.

With the compact footprint low relief buildings are used behind the depot to suggest a bigger world outside of the compact baseboard, while a 2ft long off-scene storage yard allows locos to arrive and depart from Talbot Lane.

Talbot Lane originally featured in HM142.

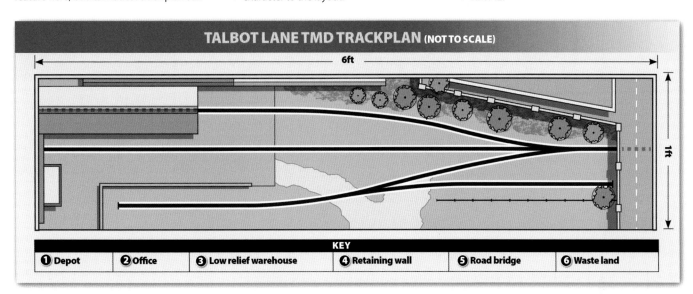

TALBOT LANE TMD TRACKPLAN (NOT TO SCALE)

6ft / 1ft

KEY

❶ Depot	❷ Office	❸ Low relief warehouse	❹ Retaining wall	❺ Road bridge	❻ Waste land

8. Old Oak Bridge

Builder: Garry Payne
Gauge: 'OO' gauge
Period: 1980s

As Garry Payne's Old Oak Bridge layout shows, it's not just about what is outside the depot – the interior is just as important. This single-track depot forms part of Garry's busy London suburb's theme 'OO' gauge layout and the interior is fully detailed with a Class 08 receiving an overhaul plus paint cans, ladders, staff, tools, steps and more. It's an enthralling scene and one which Garry can enjoy by simply lifting the building off the layout to see the interior he has created.

Old Oak Bridge originally featured in HM179. ■

Below: **Talbot Lane is a compact depot scene with a single track building. Lineside details, lighting and motive power bring it to life.**

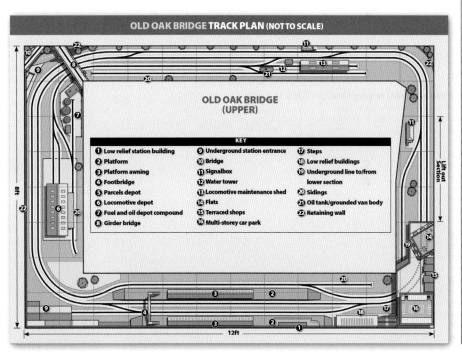

OLD OAK BRIDGE TRACK PLAN (NOT TO SCALE)

OLD OAK BRIDGE (UPPER)

KEY

❶ Low relief station building	❾ Underground station entrance	⓱ Steps
❷ Platform	❿ Bridge	⓲ Low relief buildings
❸ Platform awning	⓫ Signalbox	⓳ Underground line to/from lower section
❹ Footbridge	⓬ Water tower	⓴ Sidings
❺ Parcels depot	⓭ Locomotive maintenance shed	㉑ Oil tank/grounded van body
❻ Locomotive depot	⓮ Flats	㉒ Retaining wall
❼ Fuel and oil depot compound	⓯ Terraced shops	
❽ Girder bridge	⓰ Multi-storey car park	

It's not just external detail which counts in depot scene – building interiors can be fully furnished too with the huge array of laser cut and 3D printed products now available to model everything from spanners and hammers to paint tins and gas cylinders.

THE 1923 GROUPING
100 YEARS ON

While Britain's railway system was built in an era of optimism, which promised unlimited profits, it soon became apparent that the opposite was the case. As a result, various Governments had to make several interventions to avoid catastrophic financial failure, with the first of these being in 1923, when what is now termed the Grouping took place. **EVAN GREEN-HUGHES** explains.

The Southern Railway's Bulleid 'Q1' 0-6-0s were built in the Second World War with power and ease of maintenance as a priority. In 1947 'Q1' C15 stands in Chichester Yard with a mixed freight.
Dave Cobbe Collection/Railphotoprint.uk

January 1, 1923 was a momentous day in the history of Britain's railways for it was then that the railway lines, land, locomotives, carriages, trucks, and staff of more than 120 nominally independent companies were thrown together into four large groups that would from then on, it was hoped, run the system in a much more economical manner than had been possible previously.

The new companies, which like their predecessors would be privately-owned, would each control a very large slice of the country. In the case of the Great Western Railway (GWR) this would include much of the west as well as most of Wales, the London and North Eastern Railway (LNER) would have the East Coast Main Line and most of the tracks to the east of the country, the London, Midland and Scottish Railway (LMS) would take the West Coast Main Line as well as routes to the north-west, while the Southern Railway (SR) would have all the lines south of London as well as some towards the south west. Scotland was to be shared out between the LMS and the LNER.

Included in this share-out were some very profitable lines, particularly the older trunk routes, but each of the new companies also had a large portfolio of secondary and branch lines, many of which had been built to compete with each other,

while freight services ranged from profitable bulk minerals to extremely time-consuming and expensive to staff local goods trains, serving remote country villages and small towns that hardly drummed up enough money to pay the coal bill for the locomotives, let alone make any contribution to the cost of running the line itself.

Because of the recent war the system was also very run down. Little had been spent on maintenance during the hostilities, while much of the railway's manufacturing and repair base had been turned over to war work. The problems were immense, but it was felt they would be better solved by working together, rather than by competing.

Changing priorities

The UK's railway system had been allowed to develop in a piece-meal fashion, rather than to a central plan, contrary to the policy in many other countries. The reasons for this go back to the first railways, which were developed to satisfy local need, rather than as part of a wider transport need, while the pioneering engineering aspects were worked out on the job rather than as part of an established set of standards.

On the continent the railway system was more closely planned, but this was mainly with an eye

towards the strategic importance of the system should war break out at some time in the future. A slightly later start also meant that existing engineering standards could be imported from England, where it all began.

Britain's railway system had grown very quickly by the early 1840s and only some 15 years after the Stockton and Darlington ran its first trains the country had more than 2,000 miles of track, with the companies owning the system taking in around £4m, worth about £500m at today's prices, each year. Some railway companies were paying their shareholders annual dividends of as much as 15%, a deal that proved so tempting that everyone wanted a slice of the action. This in turn led to the 'railway mania' of 1844-1847 during which lines were built to virtually every corner of the country, whether there was a realistic demand for them or not, and in some cases led to more than one company building almost identical routes in competition with each other. Without any form of overall control things got quite out of hand, with the result that Parliament was being asked to approve a huge number of lines that together had a financial tag of six times the gross national product!

While the majority of these schemes passed the lawmakers relatively easily there was some discontent in the corridors of power »

The 1923 Grouping brought more than 120 railway companies together into four companies. Initially pre-grouping locomotives and rolling stock where still in the limelight, as shown by LNER 'D41' 4-4-0 6901 at Ferryhill Junction, Aberdeen, in 1927 as it leads a collection of -pre-grouping coaches on the Ballater train.
Railphotoprints.uk

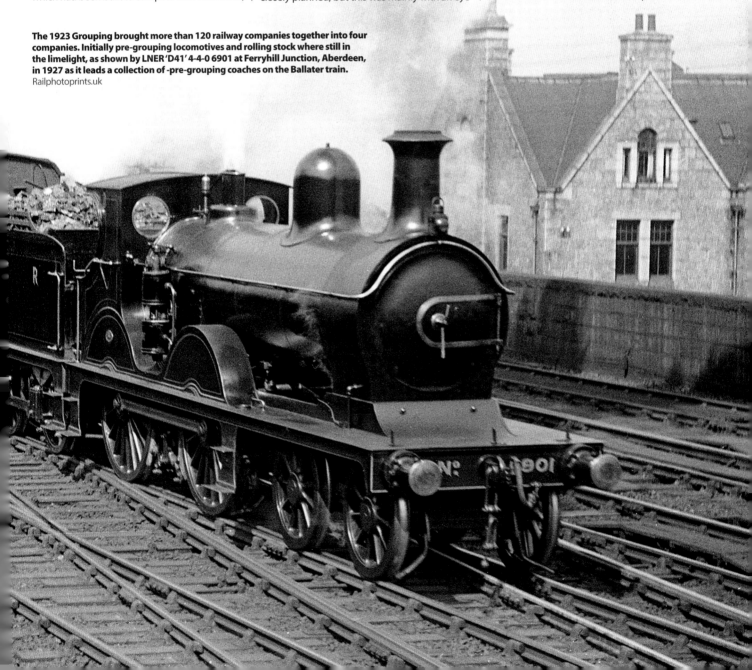

concerning wasteful competition and the long-term sustainability of the network. Legislation attempting to control the railway industry was first passed in 1839, with the private companies being overseen by a new section at the Department of Trade, but this was largely ignored so in 1844 future Prime Minister William Gladstone, then President of the Board, proposed the introduction of a law that would enable the Government to take over any railway company that did not comply with the regulations. This was the first piece of legislation that gave the Government any influence over the private companies and was, in fact, a watered-down version of a proposal that might have seen the system nationalised. Despite this, what became the 1844 Railway Regulation Act has since become more well-known for imposing on rail operators a requirement to run at least one third class train, stopping at every station, every weekday and at a speed of not less than 20mph.

Problems looming

One result of the 1844 Act was a vast increase in the numbers of Third Class passengers using the railway and over time this led to an improvement in the conditions offered to such travellers, with fully enclosed coaches, better seats and other upgrades appearing over the following 30 years or so. Unfortunately, this upgrade also brought with it an increase in operating costs, with these rising steadily until by the turn of the century more than half of each railway's income was going straight out of the door in direct operating expenses. By then another issue was the efficiency of railways varied widely from company to company. The North Eastern Railway was considered to be one of the better ones, and was considered to be extremely efficient, while at the other end of the scale the board of the Great Central Railway was frequently taken to task by its shareholders, who never saw a return on their money, which they felt had been wasted on expansionist schemes such as the London extension.

The inefficiencies of the British railway system spread far further than the individual companies themselves, for the disjointed nature of the network brought with it problems where the services of more than one company overlapped or where passengers or freight had to be carried over more than one line. In 1842 an organisation called the Railway Clearing House (RCH) was set up, largely at the behest of the London and Birmingham Railway, and this would work out in such circumstances what proportion of a fare or tariff should go to each operator. Over a period of time the RCH extended its activities to include suggesting common practices and its independence was secured in 1850 by an act of Parliament.

After eight decades Britain's railway network consisted of more than 20,000 miles of track, with about a quarter of that constructed in the latter half of the 19th century when most of the major towns and cities had already been rail connected.

Some of the companies were very small, having constructed light railways to serve a particular area, and none of these seemed able to pay anything back to their shareholders, while those which today have become household names also varied greatly in size and scope. The largest by track miles was the GWR, which was about 22 times larger than the Taff Vale Railway,

while the London and North Western, which had the biggest income, was taking about 19 times as much as the little Taff Vale. Use of the system varied too, with the South Eastern Railway receiving three quarters of its income from passengers, which was almost the same proportion as the Taff Vale took from freight.

While these statistics varied a great deal there was one trend that was shared by the whole railway network and that was of a decline in profitability. So much so that by the 1890s returns from railway investment were being overtaken by potential earnings from other sectors, which in turn made attracting further investment difficult. Existing shareholders did continue to get paid out, but their investments were declining in value and the returns were very poor. Fund managers naturally turned away from railways, but there was sufficient optimism and the result of that was that the situation did not become critical.

War changes everything

And so it may have remained had the world not been plunged into the First World War, which broke out in 1914. In fact, there had been concerns about the political state of Europe since around 1911 and one of the precautionary steps taken had been to form a

Gresley 'B17/4' 4-6-0 2851 *Derby County* climbs through Neepsend as it leaves Sheffield in 1936 with an excursion. The LNER made great strides in improving passenger accommodation during the 'Big Four' era with this train being formed of LNER Tourist stock that was introduced to accommodate excursion trains. Railphotoprints.uk

Railway Executive Committee, which brought together the managers of many of the leading companies with the intention of coming up with a scheme that would enable the whole system to work as if it was one in the event of a national emergency. That emergency came on August 4 1914 when Britain declared war on Germany and by midnight on that day the Government had taken control of the railway system, using powers granted by the 1871 Regulation of the Forces Act.

The financial provisions of the takeover were somewhat strange in that the Government decided that all war traffic should be carried by the railways free of charge, but by way of compensation the companies would receive an income equivalent to that received in 1913. The problem with this arrangement was that traffic multiplied considerably while income was held at pre-war levels, at a time when inflation was rampant. While the railways rallied to the challenge, for instance by running 334 troop trains to Southampton within eight days, there was insufficient money coming in to provide for the maintenance and renewals that were required. The only solution available to managers was to defer repairs and to make do and mend, a situation not assisted by many of the railways' works being turned over to producing armaments for the war effort. The situation was not helped when a great many railwaymen volunteered to join the forces, leaving a skill void, while many others were later sent over to France to assist in the running of the railways there that were supplying front line troops. The conflict lasted for four years and at the end of it the railway, which had been not very profitable at the outbreak, was on its knees.

The war had made it very clear that the previous system of allowing unlimited competition was in fact the road to ruin, for there was not enough »

The grouping era brought with it rapid development in motive power through the powers of the 'Big Four'. The ultimate in Southern Railway locomotive design was the 'Merchant Navy' class which were introduced in 1941. In 1947, the final year before nationalisation, air-smoothed 'Merchant Navy' 21C19 *French Line CGT*, powers through Vauxhall with the down 'Bournemouth Belle'. Railphotoprints.uk

The Great Western Railway had already made advances in standardised locomotive design prior to the grouping and continued to build that image from 1923 forwards. GWR Churchward 'Star' 4-6-0 4008 *Royal Star* poses outside one of Old Oak Common shed's large roundhouses on May 10 1934. Railphotoprints.uk

trade to go round in peacetime, and while many had opposed it, an element of Government control had in fact been good for the industry. Inevitably there was pressure from managers and shareholders alike for companies with common interests to be amalgamated into larger and more efficient organisations, something that had been happening since the mid-1840s alliance when the London and North Western Railway was formed and, in the process, assumed control of the main routes from London to Birmingham and the north west. Further route mileage was added in 1922 when the Lancashire and Yorkshire Railway became part of the same company.

Amalgamation

While it was obvious to most people that the railway system could not continue in its present form, there was little agreement as to what should be done about it. Nationalisation had been suggested on and off since 1864 but its adoption was not widely supported, largely because it would remove all competition, something that politicians and managers alike felt was necessary.

In 1919 the Government of the day formed the Ministry of Transport under the guidance of Conservative Minister Eric Geddes, with the new organisation being tasked with coming up with suggestions as to how the railway

system should be managed. Three different plans were subsequently laid before a cabinet meeting in June 1920, the first was that the system should become completely state owned and run, the second was that the current 120 companies should be allowed to continue without interference, while the third was a sort of combination of the two in which companies would be forced to amalgamate into bigger groups while at the same time staying within the private sector. The politicians of the day went for this final option, which was seen as a way of providing an efficient railway system without it having to be directly funded by the Government.

While there was general agreement as to how the railways should be restructured the same was not true as regards the actual detail. The original proposals contained provision for a separate company to manage Scotland's railways, while there was also pressure for an organisation that would bring together all the railways serving London, including the tube. Neither of these found enough support for them to be progressed, but it is interesting to note that the current franchise system has companies that cover both these geographical areas in more or less the same way as had been suggested in 1919.

Eric Geddes felt that the reorganisation should have gone further, and he favoured a much

more integrated transport system, which would have included road transport, whereas what actually happened was that the new Ministry of Transport granted a great deal of freedom to the growing road haulage sector, which was later to adversely affect the railways.

The 1921 Railways Act took the railways out of Government control, but at the same time it placed unreasonable obligations on the companies that did not spill over to other forms of transport. One of these was the creation of a Railway Rates Tribunal that was set up to fix standard tariffs for freight. From then on, the companies were obliged to carry any freight that was offered at pre-determined rates irrespective of what it cost to do the job. As these rates were published then any competitor had no problems with cherry picking the best jobs and quoting a cheaper rate, leaving the more difficult and unprofitable work for the railways to pick up.

So, hampered by a raft of new and restrictive legislation, the 120 companies were brought together in a series of forced marriages, something that was not made any easier because many of those involved had not been

During the late 1920s there was great competition between the 'Big Four' railway companies for publicity with the GWR and SR vying for the most powerful locomotive. The GWR's 'King' 4-6-0 was the company's answer to the Southern's 'Lord Nelson' class which had previously beaten the GWR 'Castle' to the title – at least until more powerful locomotives came into service in the mid-1930s. GWR 'King' 6001 *King Edward VII* passes through Taplow in 1938 with a West of England service. C.R.L Coles/Dave Cobbe Collection/Railphotoprints.uk

The Great Western Railway already had a significant stronghold in the south west, but the grouping brought its connecting railways into its control as well. In 1930 Churchward 'Saint' 4-6-0 2982 *Lalla Rookh* leaves Dawlish with an up express. Railphotoprints.uk

consulted at all during the process. Perhaps the simplest of the groups formed was the GWR, which was largely unchanged, but which had added to it a number of relatively small and local companies. The LNER had a number of large and prestigious constituents, such as the Great Northern and the North Eastern with these having their own management structures, engineering works and in some cases technical standards. The same problem affected the LMS, which was to spend years fending off tussles between Crewe and Derby as former London and North Western and Midland men continued their traditional rivalry. The most successful amalgamation was probably in the south of England where similar railways dominated by commuter traffic were more easily brought together.

However, there were also some serious anomalies, particularly where a company had built lines deep into a competitor's territory. A good example of this was the Great Central, which rivalled the Midland Main Line and largely ran in the same territory, yet which became part of the London and North Eastern largely due to its origins in the north with its line across the Pennines. **》**

With what appears to be the driver and fireman straining to move the turntable, Gresley 'P2' 2-8-2 2002 *Earl Marischal* is turned at Aberdeen Ferryhill in 1935. These giants of the LNER locomotive fleet were later rebuilt as 4-6-2s under Edward Thompson. Railphotoprints.uk

Exclusions

Although the grouping was meant to be all-encompassing, several lines were not included. The Midland and Great Northern Joint, the Cheshire Lines and the Somerset and Dorset had been jointly owned by more than one railway company and remained so after the Grouping. Tube lines and tramways were also exempt, but perhaps the most peculiar omissions were a number of light railways which presumably no one wanted. These included several that were under the control of Colonel HF Stephens, such as the Kent and East Sussex and the Rye and Camber Tramway, which somehow, he managed to keep control of. Also excluded were several narrow-gauge railways, such as the Tal-y-llyn, which had been independent and remained so, while others such as the Welshpool and Llanfair and the Vale of Rheidol were swallowed up.

Of interest was the LMS, which became the only one that was to serve Northern Ireland, as it acquired the Belfast and Northern Counties Railway system, which had been part of the Midland since 1903, with 201 miles of Irish standard gauge track as well as another 63 miles of 3ft gauge line.

Despite the difficulties, once the amalgamation began to settle down, the advantages hoped for began to become apparent. There were considerable savings due to an ability to introduce standard types of rolling stock, which could be made in bulk at the larger works, while a better quality of management was introduced on some of the lines that had up to that point not had leadership of a sufficient calibre. A great deal of time and money was saved as the necessity of accounting for cross-company traffic disappeared and there were savings to be had in bulk purchasing and middle management costs. However, one aspect that had not been foreseen was the huge increase in wages awarded to railwaymen following industrial action in 1919, which culminated in a strike. The settlement included the award of an eight-hour working day which had the effect of dramatically increasing the cost of running the system

Other issues and costs

Unfortunately, the country was soon to be hit by a recession, which derailed many of

Amalgamation of the Midland Railway into the newly formed London Midland and Scottish Railway brought with it a myriad of smaller locomotive types following the outgoing railway's policy which included the '2P' 4-4-0s. In 1933 '2P' 650 departs Glasgow St Enoch with a local service. Railphotoprints.uk

the plans that had been made for the newly amalgamated companies. Investment, which it was hoped would have been reinvigorated, continued to be strictly limited and was largely confined to areas that could still produce a return on investment, such as those serving expanding suburban developments. In some cases, the grouping actually caused the cancellation of progressive schemes. For instance, in the area around Newcastle and Darlington where the North Eastern Railway had developed a considerable network of electrified railways, which it intended to extend onto its portion of the ECML. Even though a prototype mainline electric engine had been built, the

scheme was cancelled, and the route was then stuck with steam locos for another 40 years. The same was true of the companies that used the air brake, for this was abandoned in favour of the less efficient but more commonplace vacuum brake, a move that was to have profound effects on the development of the railways in the 1960s when the better system finally had to be adopted, at great expense.

Within a few short years it became apparent that the original calculations used to justify the Grouping were proving to be hopelessly inadequate. Freight traffic figures had been assumed to continue at pre-war levels, but the end of hostilities had seen the Government

The Gresley 'A1' class 'Pacifics' first emerged at the turn of the grouping, but soon became a mainstay of East Coast Main Line expresses. A rebuilding programme started in 1928 to improve their efficiency. On May 13 1939 a grimy 'A3' 2599 *Book Law* storms north from Potters Bar with a service for Newcastle. George C. Lander/Railphotoprints.uk

Former Highland Railway 'Castle' 4-6-0 14692 *Darnaway Castle* departs from Inverness with a southbound Highland Line service during 1935. The Scottish region was divided between the LMS (western Scotland) and LNER (eastern Scotland) at the 1923 Grouping. Railphotoprints.uk

release 60,000 motor lorries in cut-price deals. Many of these were snapped up by ex-servicemen anxious to set up their own haulage companies, and who were prepared to work hard to make their businesses work. The number of commercial lorries rose from 82,000 to 151,000 in the time that it took to arrange the grouping of the railway companies and their use, particularly in rural areas, put great pressure on the railway system, much of which then proved to be uneconomic.

Higher wage costs were also eating into the efficiencies that the new companies had hoped to make. Industrial action continued throughout the early 1920s in the country in general and largely centred round a reduction in wages in mining and culminated in the General Strike of

1926. This caused considerable damage to the network, mainly from the loss of traffic that was occasioned due to customers finding alternative methods of transport while railwaymen were on strike. Things were so bad that many did not return to work immediately, only being called back up as traffic began to return.

It took several years before the new companies achieved their aim of providing a cost-efficient network, the LMS brought in a management structure of American origin and eventually hired staff from outside to end the internal rivalry, the LNER adopted a regional management system and provided for the future by creating a traffic apprenticeship scheme, the SR became a world leader in the use of public relations and produced an impressive management structure

under Sir Herbert Walker. The GWR became famous for creating its fleet of standardised locos, carriages, and even prefabricated structures. The hopes of those who had proposed amalgamation were being fulfilled on one hand, but the unforeseen aspects of rising costs and declining traffic were equally quickly removing the effects of those advantages.

In the event there were to be a few spectacular years for the new 'Big Four' companies during the 1930s when it seemed as if, at last, Britain's railways would finally be back on their feet. Unfortunately, another conflict was looming, and it was coupled with increasing competition from outside, that was to eventually kill off the amalgamated companies, only 25 years after they were formed. ∎

Stanier's motive power for the LMS continued develop steam technology while taking ideas from his time working at Swindon Works for the Great Western Railway. Stanier 'Jubilee' 4-6-0 5737 *Atlas* passes Tring Summit during 1939 with a Euston to Birmingham service. C.R.L Coles/Dave Cobbe collection/Railphotoprints.uk

BR EE TYPE 3/CLASS 37
1:76.2 SCALE/OO GAUGE

THE VERY BEST FOR A LOT LESS!

They say imitation is the sincerest form of flattery so let the Battle of Glen Fruin commence! The Accurascale 37043 alongside its stablemates in run one signifies the greatest variations in Class 37 models to date, and we're only getting started. Check your local stockist for availability, or pre-order direct with very limited numbers remaining in stock.

Locoman sound for the HORNBY '9F'

The arrival of Hornby's all-new and stunning model of the BR '9F' 2-10-0 provided a sound installation project too good to resist. **MIKE WILD** shows how you can install sound into the Hornby '9F' as designed and with optional extras.

EXCLUSIVE VIDEO ONLINE!
WWW.KEYMODELWORLD.COM
SEE IT IN ACTION

A s soon as we opened up the first of the all-new Hornby '9F' 2-10-0s we knew it was going to be something special and, at the same time, that we had to add digital sound to one of these impressive 'OO' gauge models.

The first batch arrived in September 2022 and models 92167 with a BR1K tender featuring a mechanical stoker, 92194 with a larger BR1F tender and 92220 *Evening Star* with a BR1G tender. All three versions are richly detailed and include elements specific to each locomotive as well as being equipped with a 21-pin decoder socket, space for a 15mm x 11mm cube speaker plus permanently illuminated firebox flicker in the firebox, which works on digital and analogue layouts without any further modification.

Hornby's association with the 1954-introduced BR '9Fs' goes back to 1971 when Tri-ang Hornby announced the first ready-to-run model of these large ten-coupled freight locomotives. Since then the '9F' has been a permanent resident of the Hornby catalogue with a number of revisions following the initial release, including replacement of the tender drive mechanism with a locomotive based drive system, adding an 8-pin decoder and creation of a RailRoad only model of the Crosti '9F's that had Franco Crosti boilers and side exhausts.

However, while there has been a high detail model of the '9F' available from Bachmann for 'OO' gauge since 2006, there was room for improvement

TOOLS

- » Soldering iron
- » Solder
- » Wire strippers
- » Fine scissors
- » Small crosshead screwdriver
- » Small flatblade screwdriver
- » Superglue
- » Black Tack
- » Insulation tape

Hornby's new BR '9F' 2-10-0 is an impressive addition to its collection, and even more so with authentic sound. Our completed model has twin speakers and function-controlled firebox flicker.

and Hornby saw that potential with its 2021 catalogue announcement, which included an all-new model of BR's final build of steam locomotives.

The BR Standard locomotives have been well done by Hornby in the past, with its repertoire including the 'Britannia', 'Clan' and *Duke of Gloucester* 4-6-2s and the BR '4MT' 4-6-0, while the BR '2MT' 2-6-0 is also on the way from Hornby too. The '9Fs' arrival is fully detailed in HM185 as well as online at *www.keymodelworld. com/riddles-br-9f-2-10-0* where you can read our full review, class history and more.

Here we will focus on our '9F' sound installation process. We have split this guide into two – part one follows the sound installation as intended by Hornby, with the addition of a Locoman Sounds '9F' sound profile loaded onto a Doehler & Haass 21-pin SD21A decoder coupled to a 15mm x 11mm cube speaker fitted to the sound

chamber provided in the tender. The second part is more advanced and sees the addition of a second speaker in the smokebox as well as separating the firebox flicker from the track feed so that it can be controlled from a function button in tandem with the coal shovelling sound. This also means the firebox flicker works on demand, rather than permanently, which is realistic and provides additional functional value.

The second phase of the sound installation does require greater soldering skills to complete, but the results are well worth the extra effort as you can here in our sound demonstration video online at *www.keymodelworld.com/digital-sound*.

The following step by step guide shows how we did carried out the installation for the Hornby '9F' both as designed and with the addition of a second speaker and independently controlled firebox flicker. ∎

WHAT WE USED

Product	Supplier	Cat No.
BR '9F' 2-10-0 92194, BR black	*www.hornby.com*	R3987
Rail Exclusive 15mm x 11m cube speaker	*www.digitrains.co.uk*	SP15x11x12
Rail Exclusive 18mm x 13mm cube speaker	*www.digitrains.co.uk*	SP18x13x13
D&H SD21A-4 21-pin sound decoder	*www.locomansounds.com*	SD21A-4
BR 9F sound profile	*www.locomansounds.com*	9F sound

LOCOMAN SOUNDS BR '9F' 2-10-0 SOUND FILE

F0	Lights on/off (if fitted)
F1	Sound on/off
F2	Variable whistle
F3	Short whistle
F4	Active brake
F5	Cylinder draincocks
F6	Fancy whistle
F7	Guard's whistle (stationary), flange squeal (moving)
F8	Wagon buffer clashing
F9	Forced coasting
F10	Coal shovelling and firebox flicker (Aux 1/Aux 3)
F11	Injector
F12	Coach door slams (stationary)
F13	Coupling sound (and Aux 6)
F14	Whistle with echo
F15	Safety valves
F16	Water filling (stationary)
F17	Shunting mode
F18	Volume up
F19	Volume down
F20	Aux 2/Aux 4
F21	Momentum off
F22	No brake squeal
F23	Sound fader
F24	Heavy exhaust
F25	Aux 5
F26	Reserved
F27	Light dimming (if fitted)
F28	Reserved

Note 1: Aux 1 is for use with flickering LEDs, Aux 3 provides a flicker effect for non-flickering LEDs.

Note 2: Aux 4 is preset for a Seuthe smoke generator.

STEP BY STEP **INSTALLING DIGITAL SOUND IN A HORNBY BR '9F'**

1 Hornby's all-new model of the BR '9F' 2-10-0 arrived in September 2022 and offers a stunning replica of these impressive steam locomotives. Hornby has designed it with sound in mind, but there is more that can be done – as we will show.

2 In the first part of this guide up to Step 11 we will show the model has been designed for sound installation. To start unplug the four-pin connector between the locomotive and tender using a Hornby X6468 plug removal tool.

3 Next the slotted screw that holds the tender drawbar in place can be released to allow the locomotive and tender to be separated. We find this makes it easier to work on the model, rather than leaving the tender and loco connected.

4 If you prefer you could omit separating the loco and tender, but once you have made these two simple steps to do so you will find it much easier to carry out the sound installation

5 The tender body is held in place with two screws, which are found just behind and above the rear brake shoes. Undo both of these and set them aside safely for use in reassembly later.

6 Inside the tender Hornby has fitted a 21-pin decoder socket and space for a single 15mm x 11mm cube speaker in a specially designed 'sound chamber'.

7 Our decoder for this project is a Doehler & Haass 21-pin chip supplied by Locoman Sounds with the latest '9F' sound project loaded onto it. The speaker is a Rail Exclusive 15mm x 11mm cube speaker that has been separated from its enclosure.

8 Speaker tabs, marked S1 and S2, are provided on the main Printed Circuit Board (PCB) beneath the original socket blank fitted by the factory to allow analogue use.

Intermediate
Beginner **SKILL LEVEL** Advanced

9 The speaker has been superglued in place with Roket Rapid adhesive for a firm seal to the sound chamber. We have also now added solder (a process called tinning) to the S1 and S2 tabs on the PCB to make connecting the speaker wires easier.

10 Next the speaker wires are soldered to the S1 and S2 tabs – polarity isn't important for a speaker making this a simple task to complete.

11 To complete the basic version of the sound installation the D&H sound chip is plugged in, meaning that you could now refit the tender body, reconnect the loco and return the '9F' to service. However, we wanted to go two steps further and add a second speaker as well as a function firebox flicker.

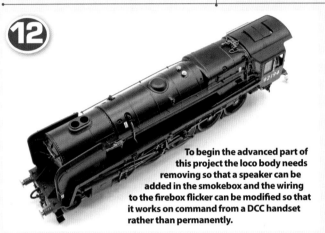

12 To begin the advanced part of this project the loco body needs removing so that a speaker can be added in the smokebox and the wiring to the firebox flicker can be modified so that it works on command from a DCC handset rather than permanently.

13 The front body securing screw is above the pony truck frame. Use a small crosshead screwdriver to release it.

14 At the rear a second screw is found above the wires from the loco to tender connection. Move these carefully for full access to the screw.

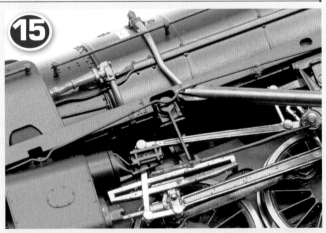

15 The last step in removal of the body is to carefully unhook the conduit from under the lubricator arms. Our project loco had had its body removed several times, which meant we had dislodged one of the brackets. We will fix this at the end of the project.

16 Inside the red and black wires are the pick-up feeds that go to the back of the firebox flicker before linking through to the loco. This gives the firebox flicker a permanent feed that we don't want, as our finished model will sync coal shovelling sounds and firebox flicker together.

The smokebox provides ample space to fit a second speaker. Our choice is a Rail Exclusive 18mm x 13mm x 13mm design that will slide neatly inside the smokebox.

17

STEP BY STEP **INSTALLING DIGITAL SOUND IN A HORNBY BR '9F'**

 18 The firebox flicker needs to be lifted from its supports on the chassis – it isn't glued in place – for access to the wires.

 **19**

The power feeds are then carefully de-soldered from the LED board, but crucially the joins between the red and black wires and their black extensions through to the tender are kept intact. Work on these one at a time, just in case they separate.

 **20**

Space is at a premium at the rear of the chassis and the amount of wire is also limited. To work around this the bare wires were very carefully wrapped in Black Tack to act as an insulator and to hold the wires in place. Note that if you don't get this right and cause a short circuit it will invalidate the warranty on your chip – work carefully and check everything.

 **21**

Having separated the firebox LED from the main track feeds, it now needs new connections to link it through to the decoder. We used black for negative and brown for the positive feed and soldered them to the original connection points on the rear of the LED circuit board.

 **22**

The firebox flicker board can now be reinstalled and the new wires can be routed through the opening at the bottom of the chassis. The wires have been cut over length to ensure we have plenty of wire to reach the decoder in the tender.

 **23**

The speaker is prepared next by adding two wires (over length) to pass through the loco boiler and into the tender. These are soldered to the outer spring tabs for a secure joint.

 **24**

To prevent any possibility of a short circuit the speaker top is wrapped with insulation tape to protect the soldered joints. In addition this makes the speaker invisible through the chimney openings when the model is viewed from above.

 **25**

The speaker wires are positioned along the inside of the loco's boiler and taped in place with insulation tape to prevent them interfering with the motor or gearbox.

 **26**

Next the speaker wires are routed through the opening at the base of the loco behind the rear driving wheel prior to reassembly of the body and chassis.

 **27**

The body is refitted in the reverse order of dismantling, taking care to ensure all the new wires pass through freely without snagging or getting caught by internal parts. If the body won't fit properly then take it off again and adjust the position of the wires.

Intermediate
Beginner **SKILL LEVEL** Advanced

28

To make way for the new speaker and firebox flicker wires to enter the tender a pair of 2mm diameter holes were drilled through the tender chassis using a pin vice. These were drilled at an angle to keep the wires away from the tender wheels and the front of the tender body.

29

The tender has now been reconnected to the loco to ensure that the new wires are cut to the right length to suit. The new pairs of wires have also now been threaded through the new holes in the tender chassis.

30

Next the black wire from the firebox flicker is connected to the Aux 1 output at the bottom of the 21-pin socket. Care is needed here to check its position in the D&H decoder manual and that the solder only contact Pin 15.

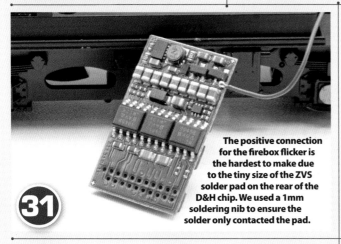

31

The positive connection for the firebox flicker is the hardest to make due to the tiny size of the ZVS solder pad on the rear of the D&H chip. We used a 1mm soldering nib to ensure the solder only contacted the pad.

The original speaker wires fitted in step 10 have been disconnected and joined to each of the speaker wires from the second speaker in the loco with solder. The wires were also reduced in length before making this connection.

32

33

To complete the soldering processes the speaker wires were re-soldered to the S1 and S2 connections on the loco's main PCB.

The final step is to refit the D&H chip from Locoman Sounds and test the locomotive's functions work as expected before refitting the tender body.

34

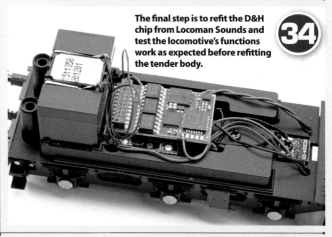

35

92194 is now complete and ready to enter service with a full suite of realistic sounds from Locoman Sounds. The firebox flicker now works with the coal shovelling sound both through Function 10 and at random in the sound project, making this an even more enjoyable loco to operate.

Masterpieces in the
GALLERY

We present a selection of the best layouts and model photography from the past 12 months in *Hornby Magazine*.

Malcolm Bentley's stunning home-based 'OO' gauge layout models Old Oak Common depot in West London when hydraulic traction was coming to the end of its rule on the Western Region. Overlooking the Pullman shed (left) and main turntable, Class 42 Warships and Class 52 Westerns dominate the scene alongside classes 22, 35 and 47. Old Oak Common featured in HM186.
Mike Wild/*Hornby Magazine*

For the second year running Pete Waterman and the Railnuts group built and displayed a huge 64ft long model of the West Coast Main Line in Chester Cathedral for Making Tracks II. This time the layout modelled the approaches to Rugby at Hillmorton Junction and the full layout featured in HM181. A Class 90 speeds north towards Rugby as an HST set heads south with a pair of Class 37s on the Northampton lines. Pete Waterman and the group will be returning to Chester Cathedral in summer 2023 with Making Tracks III. *Mike Wild/Hornby Magazine*

Collingwood is Simon Paley's latest OO gauge layout which models the third-rail network in the present-day taking inspiration from Fareham. Viewed through the unloading terminal at the aggregates yard, a Class 450 prepares to depart while a Class 66 ticks over in the yard. Collingwood featured in HM185. *Mike Wild/Hornby Magazine*

A Class 50 rounds the curve from the branch line at Boscarwen Junction with a rake of CDA china clay hoppers. This compact N gauge layout is the work of Daniel Harris and featured in HM182. *Trevor Jones/Hornby Magazine*

LAYOUT OF THE YEAR 2022 WINNER
This stunning OO gauge model of Little Bytham on the East Coast Main Line was built by Tony Wright and won the reader vote to be Layout of the Year in the 2022 Hornby Magazine Model Railway Awards. A Gresley A4 and Thompson A2/3 4-6-2 pass on the main lines while a Gresley 'J6' 0-6-0 shunts in the yard. Little Bytham featured in HM180. *Mike Wild/Hornby Magazine*

The London Underground network is the theme for Tony Dean's marvellous and compact OO gauge layout. An Ivatt 2MT 2-6-2T waits to depart with a train for the BR network while a set of Standard stock leaves the bay platform. Greenford Broadway featured in HM183. Trevor Jones/*Hornby Magazine*

Dawlish Warren is Chris Morris' latest N gauge layout which models the famous station on approach to the Devon coastline. Western D1056 *Western Sultan* powers through the centre road with an express for Penzance while holiday makers make the most of the good weather. Dawlish Warren featured in HM180. Mike Wild/*Hornby Magazine*

Southpool is Steve Johnson's evocative portrayal of the North West in the final years of steam. Stanier Duchess 46232 *Duchess of Montrose* simmers by the coaling plant in the company of a Stanier Black Five. Southpool featured in HM177. Mike Wild/*Hornby Magazine*

East London in the late 1940s is the setting for Jim and Charlie Conner's OO gauge layout. Harford Street has been through a number of rebuilds and the latest version models the railway set into the streets of the period. Harford Street featured in HM184. Trevor Jones/*Hornby Magazine*

Waldbury is Bernard Newbury's huge home-based OO gauge model railway. It models a through station set in the final years of the 'Big Four' with a leaning towards Great Western Railway and London Midland Scottish Railway motive power. Coal traffic is a signature of this layout with long rakes of private owner wagons threading through the point work and along the main lines. Here a GWR 72XX 2-8-2T draws a rake of loaded coal wagons out of the yard. Waldbury featured in HM176. *Mike Wild/Hornby Magazine*

CONSTRUCTION

SWITHLAND VIADUCT

The missing piece of the Hornby Magazine Great Central Railway layout is finally complete: Swithland Reservoir bridge. **MIKE WILD** explains how PAUL CHAPMAN'S superb scratchbuilt viaduct was installed into the layout.

EXCLUSIVE VIDEO ONLINE!
WWW.KEYMODELWORLD.COM/
BUILDING-GREAT-CENTRAL-RAILWAY
WATCH THE FULL
GCR VIDEO BUILD SERIES

O ur model of the Great Central Railway, which is now the central test track at Hornby Magazine HQ, has always been about creating a pastiche of the real railway. A scene that is believable, takes inspiration from the real location, but also uses modeller's licence to suit the shape of a continuous run model railway.

When we started planning the GCR layout the greatest challenge was fitting as many of the elements of the surviving double track section as possible into a 16ft x 8ft footprint. From the get-go it meant compromises in station length, loop length and track arrangement and also meant we had to introduce curves that aren't present on the real railway.

The resulting layout takes a journey from Quorn Magna – our classic GCR London Extension station with its island platform, road bridge entrance and simple goods yard – and then curves around the spot we had planned for our version of Swithland Reservoir which, until now, has stood completely bare. After crossing the reservoir bridge the line sweeps through Swithland Sidings, which has the gentle curves of the main line as well as a fan of sidings and a branch to Mountsorrel, though this currently reaches its limit at the end of the baseboard.

The reservoir scene has been the most challenging part to create. We made it difficult for ourselves by placing the scene on a curve, but in turn it would also create an attractive scene. This autumn we have finally brought the reservoir scene to life and in this feature we will explain how.

Starting point

The first step was the design of the board, which was completed right at the very beginning of the layout build. As we assembled the laser cut boards, we saw the potential to add a lower level section for the reservoir

The newly installed Swithland Reservoir bridge sets the scenes as BR 'Britannia' 70013 *Oliver Cromwell* sweeps round on the approach to Swithland sidings.

scene to add something different to the layout. To do so we added panels of 18mm thick Medium Density Fibreboard (MDF) to one end and side of the reservoir baseboard, which increased the overall length and width of the layout by the same amount. To ensure the whole baseboard system would still together square we added strips of 18mm thick MDF to one of the station boards at the joint as well as between the opposite end boards for consistency.

Next a new trackbed was cut from 6mm MDF which was then screwed in place at end of the reservoir board before a pair of 6mm MDF supports were added to ensure it didn't sag under the weight of passing trains. And that is how the board remained for its first two public outings at the 2021 Great Electric Train Show and the Statford Barn Model Railway Exhibition in 2022.

After we returned from the Statfold Barn event it was time to get to work on the reservoir scene and the first stage was building the bridge. To fit the scene we needed a scratchbuilt model as no commercially available product would be able to model the real viaduct at Swithland around a curve. To make the viaduct we called in the services of scratchbuilder Paul Chapman who previously built the two signal boxes for the layout. To get Paul started a paper template of the bridge deck was traced and marked up for the position of the arches and bridge opening and posted to him.

On receipt Paul set to work cutting out the deck for the bridge and working out

A Robinson 'O4' and 'WD' 2-8-0 meet on the bridge. The structure was scratchbuilt by Paul Chapman from card and plasticard and you can read the full build online at *www.keymodelworld.com*

the shapes and sizes of the components he would need for the model. Card was used for the structure overlaid with brick plasticard to create a model which replicates the real viaduct, but on a curve.

A few months later the post system delivered one carefully packed bridge to the Hornby Magazine Workshop ready for installation and, incredibly considering it had been built completely away from the workshop, it fitted with just one small modification to the MDF bridge deck on the layout. Paul had designed the bridge so that the original MDF deck could be retained, which gave the trackbed strength and allowed the bridge model not to be load bearing. You can read our full step by step modelling guide for construction of the bridge at *www.keymodelworld.com*.

Scenic process
Having checked the bridge fitted, we removed it from the scene to allow the first layer of weathering to be applied to the track. To

match the rest of the layout Humbrol No. 29 was sprayed over the double track formation to cover the sleepers and rail sides, after which the rail heads were cleaned to ensure electrical continuity for the trains.

Now the bridge could be installed for the final time, and because of its snug fit we had no need to glue it into position, particularly as the later layers of ballast glue from above and water below would hold it in place. Testing then followed to double check that different length coaches would still run around the curves on the bridge without catching the sides. The longest length tested were Hornby Mk 3 and Mk 4 75ft stock.

Forming of the landscape came next with the used of polystyrene blocks – both rescued from packaging and off-cuts of insulation – which were built up to the right height and then shaped with a hot wire cutter before any glue was applied. Doing it this way means the cutter only has to work through the polystyrene blocks and it also saves on drying times too – important

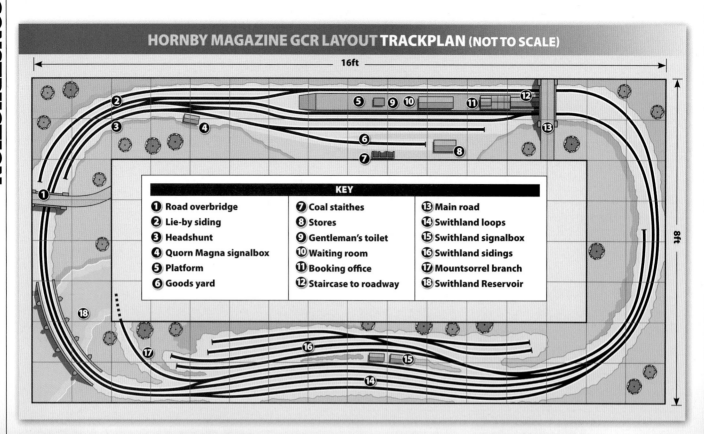

HORNBY MAGAZINE GCR LAYOUT TRACKPLAN (NOT TO SCALE)

16ft

8ft

KEY

1. Road overbridge
2. Lie-by siding
3. Headshunt
4. Quorn Magna signalbox
5. Platform
6. Goods yard
7. Coal staithes
8. Stores
9. Gentleman's toilet
10. Waiting room
11. Booking office
12. Staircase to roadway
13. Main road
14. Swithland loops
15. Swithland signalbox
16. Swithland sidings
17. Mountsorrel branch
18. Swithland Reservoir

USEFUL LINKS	
Woodland Scenics	www.bachmann.co.uk
Green Scene	www.green-scenes.co.uk
Primo Trees	www.primomodels.com
Bachmann Scenecraft	www.bachmann.co.uk
Hatton's Model Railways	www.hattons.co.uk
The Model Tree Shop	www.modeltreeshop.co.uk

when you are working to a 10-day deadline as we were at the time of the scene's construction.

The shaped polystyrene was fixed in place with neat PVA adhesive followed by layers of plaster bandage from Hobby Craft to create a hardshell landscape. As we wanted to preserve the detail of the bridge and prevent splashed of plaster, all of the bandage was laid dry and then soaked with a water mister to bond it into place over the landscape. It was then immediately painted brown using

Daler Rowney Burnt Umber acrylic to give the landscape a consistent base colour.

We now had a completed basic landform which needed to dry for at least 24 hours, so while that was happening, we ballasted the track using matching Woodland Scenics fine and medium grade Blended Gray ballasts which were mixed together prior to being applied to the trackbed loose. The ballast was then brushed carefully into place, wetted with a water mister then sealed in place with SBR

One of Hornby's new BR '9F' 2-10-0s leads a rake of Accurascale 24.5ton HUO hoppers round the curve. The water below is Woodland Scenics Realistic Water.

WHAT WE USED		
Product	Manufacturer	Cat No.
Fine blended green turf	Woodland Scenics	T1349
Light green coarse turf	Woodland Scenics	T1363
Burnt grass coarse turf	Woodland Scenics	T1362
Light green fine leaf foliage	Woodland Scenics	F1132
Medium green fine leaf foliage	Woodland Scenics	F1131
Olive green fine leaf foliage	Woodland Scenics	F1133
Purple pollen	Woodland Scenics	T4648
Red pollen	Woodland Scenics	T4647
Realistic Water	Woodland Scenics	C1211
Long summer static grass	Green Scene	
Medium summer static grass	Green Scene	
Long spring static grass	Green Scene	
Medium spring static grass	Green Scene	
Long straw static grass	Green Scene	

adhesive applied with a syringe working from the centre of the sleepers out.

Ground cover

Having left the base layers to dry thoroughly the next phase of the project was to begin building up the ground cover. First was an overall application of Woodland Scenics Blended Green fine turf to all the embankments and islands to act as a base layer to static grasses. The fine turf layer was fixed in place with PVA glue spread with a damp paint brush and once this was dry the excess material was gathered into a pot for further use.

A layer of static grass applied over diluted PVA in a 70:30 ratio with water was added next using a combination of Woodland Scenics and Green Scene grasses for variety in tone, length and colour.

The biggest single scenic element of this build was the reservoir itself and to start this process Woodland Scenics' coarse blended gray ballast

was applied loose around the footings of the bridge to represent silt being deposited by water and simulate movement in the finished scene.

Having prepared the reservoir bed, we could start pouring the reservoir using Woodland Scenics Realistic Water. This product dries clear and can be built up in layers, but as we had almost four-square feet to cover it used a full bottle for each layer allowing a minimum of 12 hours between pours. To prevent the Realistic Water running off the edge of the baseboard we added a bead of clear silicone sealant around the edge which created a raised border to the reservoir.

Care was needed to ensure full coverage from the Realistic Water and to keep the baseboard level during the drying process. We also found it handy to be able to manipulate the position of the board to flow the water around the scene to cover all areas, with such a big area to cover.

While the water was still drying we added tufts of Woodland Scenics straw fibres that were cut into 8-10mm lengths to represent long grasses growing at the edge of the water. After this it was another case of being patient to allow the water to cure fully overnight.

Final flourish

At this stage the scene was starting to become something, but the grasses were still quite basic and lacked the full depth of texture that the rest of the ground cover had around the GCR layout.

To take care of this further layers of static grass, blended green fine turf and coarse turfs were applied over the first layers of ground cover using Matt Varnish as an adhesive. This is an enjoyable and rewarding process as the layers build up quickly and you can keep adding on top of each successive layer immediate, rather than having to wait for glues to dry.

Within 30 minutes the ground cover had built up to match the original layout and we also overlaid an extra layer around the baseboard joints, feathering it in to blend the new and old together.

Completing the scene were clumps of Woodland Scenics fine leaf foliage around the base of the bridge to blend it into the ground followed by signature trees from Primo Models and 3D printed fencing from Geoscenics to separate the railway from its surrounding land.

Now we have a completed layout, but one which we would be hard pressed to say was finished. Looking around, Swithland Sidings needs more ground cover texture and a copse of trees around the Mountsorrel branch to create a visual break between the different scenes. Looking further along the sidings section more weathering would improve the scene, and we also have ideas around adding an extra feature, such as a small depot, around the short sidings to add a little more visual interest, even though it isn't part of the real scene.

Over at Quorn Magna there are three main jobs on the list including recovering of the yard surfaces with Geoscenics potholed road products to enhance the surface, while the platforms need sanding and repainting, and the lamps need wiring up too. Finger's crossed we'll have all that done soon and the GCR layout really will be complete as the backdrop to the Hornby Magazine and KeyModelWorld demonstration videos.

Heavy freight 2-8-0s cross on the viaduct. The original MDF deck cut as part of the baseboard modifications still provides the trackbed for the Peco code 75 bullhead track.

CONSTRUCTION

STEP BY STEP **BUILDING SWITHLAND RESERVOIR IN 'OO' GAUGE**

1

The reservoir scene has been pending construction since we started building the GCR layout in 2020. The baseboard was modified to be lower at the start of the build to make way for the future reservoir scene.

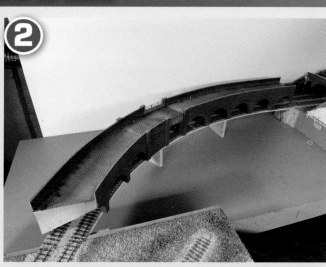

2

Arrival of the scratchbuilt bridge from Paul Chapman shortly before the 2022 Great Electric Train Show prompted us to swing into action to complete the scene. A first test showed that the bridge fitted the shape of the trackbed with one small modification to narrow the width of the original MDF trackbed at one point.

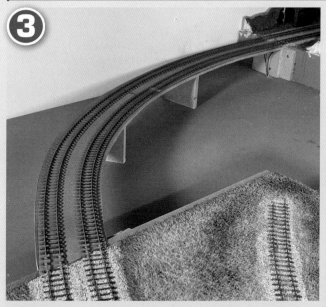

3

Next the track was given a base layer of weathering to match the rest of the layout using Humbrol No. 29 from an aerosol spray can – a quick and effective base colour that dries in ten minutes.

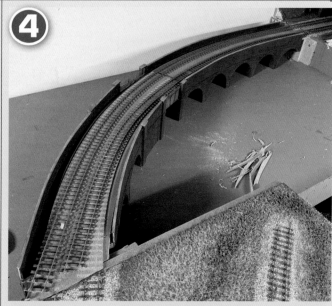

4

To install the bridge the track had to be lifted at the baseboard joint to allow the MDF trackbed to be lifted. With the trackbed lifted at one end the new bridge slid underneath and fitted perfectly.

5

A few minutes later and the track had been restored to its original position allowing clearance tests to take place with a selection of trains.

6

Landscaping starts with polystyrene blocks that were cut to shape with a hot wire cutter prior to being glued in place. The hot wire cutter makes shaping of polystyrene a much cleaner process.

Intermediate
Beginner **SKILL LEVEL** Advanced

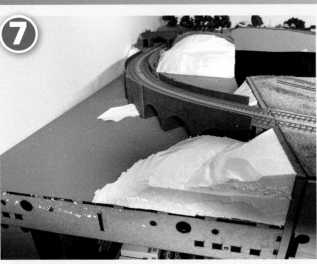

7

The landscape was built up around the bridge to lead down to the waters edge from the main baseboard height. Once shaped with the hot wire cutter the blocks were glued in place with PVA wood glue.

8

Plaster bandage was added over the polystyrene blocks to create a hardshell. To keep the process as clean as possible the strips of plaster bandage were laid dry and then wetted with a water mister. As soon as this process was completed the whole landscape was painted dark brown with Daler Rowney Burnt Umber acrylic.

9

Ballasting of the main lines followed using a combination of Woodland Scenics fine and medium grade Blended Gray ballasts. Once the ballast was brushed into place it was wetted with a water mister then set in place with SBR adhesive.

10

A base layer of Woodland Scenics blended green fine turf was added the grass bank next to start the ground cover process.

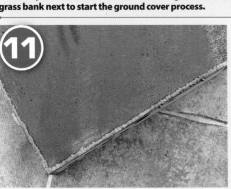

11

Preparations for the Woodland Scenics Realistic Water start with a bead of clear silicone around the edge of the baseboard. Once dry this will prevent the Realistic Water from running off the baseboard during application.

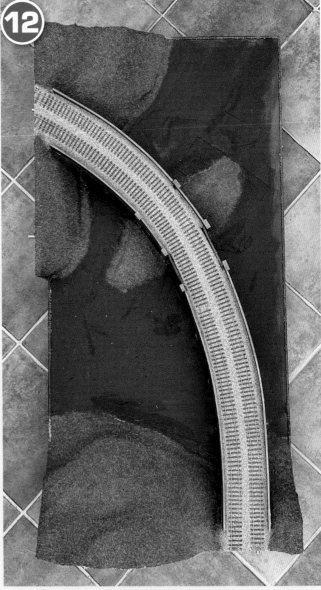

12

A first layer of static grass was applied next over the top of the initial fine blended turf layer. This static grass layer is held in place with a 70:30 ratio of PVA to water.

STEP BY STEP | **BUILDING SWITHLAND RESERVOIR IN 'OO' GAUGE**

As a final step before pouring the water we added Woodland Scenics' coarse blended gray ballast around the footings for the viaduct to suggest a build-up of silt as well as movement in the water.

Woodland Scenics' Realistic Water can be poured direct from the bottle. With such a large area – almost four-square feet – each layer took a full bottle of the product. To ensure the water covered the entire board we tilted the board immediately following application to move the Realistic Water to all areas before leaving it level to dry.

To add a little detail at the water's edge, tufts of Woodland Scenics straw were cut to 8-10mm lengths and set into the Realistic Water while it was still drying. These will represent long grasses.

As the Realistic Water dries it contracts which is why multiple layers are needed to build up the depth of the water. This is the finished effect of one layer across the reservoir base – more are needed.

Two more pours later and the reservoir is looking much deeper. Woodland Scenics' dead wood has been added around the edge of the water too for a little extra detail.

Once the water had set multiple layers of static grass, fine blended turf and coarse turf were applied over the top of the base layers using Matt Varnish as an adhesive. Varnish is sprayed on before and after each layer to both stick and seal the scenic material in place.

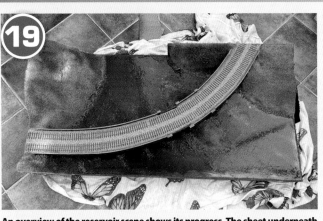

An overview of the reservoir scene shows its progress. The sheet underneath was positioned to collect any run off of Realistic Water – it's amazing how it always finds a way through – to prevent the water reaching the floor below.

Reunited with the main layout the reservoir scene is taking shape and is now ready for the addition of final details including trees and bushes.

Woodland Scenics' fine leaf foliage blends the bridge into the scenery while Geoscenics' fencing adds a boundary between railway and non-railway land.

Primo Models' trees add signature specimens to the scene and add much needed height around the railway.

Super-detailed
NORTH EASTERN
WORKHORSE

Even modelling examples of ubiquitous steam locomotive types can present unique challenges for detailing, as **RICHARD HALL** demonstrates by comprehensively reworking Oxford Rail's J27 into 65894 as currently preserved.

Until the end of North Eastern steam in 1967, the region featured a fascinating range of traffic and motive power, consequentially becoming a popular modelling subject. The success of Hornby's 'Q6' 0-8-0 in 2016 increased calls for a ready-to-run model of the stablemate 'J27', which was fulfilled in

2019 by Oxford Rail announcing the North Eastern Railway 'P3' 0-6-0, later classified 'J27' under the LNER.

The only survivor of the once-numerous 'J27' class, 65894, was preserved by the North Eastern Locomotive Preservation Group (NELPG), alongside 'Q6' 63395, and has proven a

TOOLS

- » Cotton buds
- » Cocktail sticks
- » Masking tape
- » Scalpel
- » Photoetch cutters
- » Photo etch folder
- » Handrail bending jig
- » Flat nosed pilers
- » Xuron sprue cutters
- » Tweezers
- » Steel rules
- » Assorted files & sanding sticks
- » Paint brushes (sizes 000 – 3)
- » Soldering iron, flux & solder
- » Micro Phillips screwdriver set

highly popular and capable locomotive both at the North Yorkshire Moors Railway (NYMR) and other heritage lines. As a result of 65894 being refitted with a non-superheated (saturated) boiler in 1966, the locomotive is fitted with a lower superheated 'J27' dome, but on a non-superheated boiler and shorter smokebox: this unique detail variation makes creating an accurate as-preserved model of 65894 a more involved process.

Being produced at a relatively affordable price point, Oxford's rendition of the 'J27' captures the character of the class, but does feature drawbacks, predominantly in terms of shape and detail omissions. Oxford Rail's current tooling depicts the non-superheated 'J27s', with the late crest model of 65814 providing the best starting point for creating 65894.

The most significant improvements made during this project were achieved using a selection of White metal and brass detail components from Dave Bradwell, allowing for the replacement of the smokebox door, chimney, tender axel boxes and lowered dome. While Dave Bradwell's complete 'J27' kit remains a highly reputable model for the class, the cast detailing parts that are retained in very limited quantities allows for any Oxford 'J27' to be markedly improved.

Scratch building also played a significant role in the project; constructing new three-rail tender coal rails presented the most challenging part, where a temperature-controlled soldering iron was vital in allowing for minute changes to alignment. The cab side windows can similarly be improved, with the top of the windows being carefully sanded into a more accurate elliptical curve, before adding new beading and scratch-built sliding windowpanes.

With the model of 65894 complete, my thanks to Declan Hargreaves for use of his photographs of the real 65894 on the NYMR in the same condition as replicated on this model. However, my particular thanks to Dave Bradwell for his

help with the project, as while my intention remains to build the full 'J27' kit from his range, the new cast components were invaluable and made the largest difference to the outcome of the model.

Replicating 65894 took around 28 hours of work and proved a fantastic project for sharpening skills, especially with soldering brass.

The base model by Oxford Rail is certainly ripe for detailing and improvement, and while this step-by-step guide depicts the more extreme degree of additions for 65894 as currently preserved, even renumbering and weathering can make a marked improvement to the model and can be applied to all periods of this ubiquitous class. ∎

WHAT WE USED		
Product	**Supplier**	**Cat No.**
10" Off-white cabside numbering transfers	www.fox-transfers.co.uk	FRH4008
British Railways late Lion and Wheel crests	www.fox-transfers.co.uk	FRH4014/1
LNER Etched brass works plates	www.fox-transfers.co.uk	See text
1960s electrification flashes	www.railtec-models.co.uk	4mm-1056
BR White Smokebox numbering	www.railtec-models.co.uk	4mm-4100
Custom 3D shed code transfer (52G)	www.railtec-models.co.uk	4mm-9095
LNER/BR(E) Loco Lamps	www.modelu3d.co.uk	2060
Plasticard sheet – 0110/0120/0130/0160	www.slatersplasticard.com	Various
Plasticard rod sections	www.slatersplasticard.com	Various
1.5mm x 0.5mm brass half round rod	www.eileensemporium.com	D01005E
0.4mm flexible blackened copper wire	www.amazon.com	
0.5mm brass rod	www.albionalloys.com	BR1
1.0mm brass rod	www.albionalloys.com	BW10 3mm
No 46 Phosphor Bronze guitar string	www.amazon.com	PO1846
Acrylic paints & weathering powders	uk.humbrol.com	Various
Railmatch Acrylic paints & varnishes	www.howesmodels.co.uk	Various
Railmatch Enamel spray & gloss varnish	www.howesmodels.co.uk	See text
Tamiya Panel line accent (black)	www.amazon.co.uk	87131
99.8% Isopropyl Alcohol	www.amazon.co.uk	
6mm Tamiya masking tape	www.tamiya.com	87030
Deluxe Materials Plastic Magic	www.deluxematerials.co.uk	AD77
Deluxe Materials Glue 'n glaze	www.deluxematerials.co.uk	AD55
Scale screw link couplings	www.hornby.com	R7200
Zimo 21-pin MTC DCC Decoder	www.agrmodelrailwaystore.co.uk	MX638D

With a range of detailing opportunities to suit many skill levels, Oxford Rail's J27 presents a locomotive perfect for improvement, and as demonstrated in this guide, can be effectively super detailed into the sole preserved example.

The tender of 65894 featured key improvements that can be applied to any J27 model, and all contribute towards achieving a more durable and accurate model.

STEP BY STEP DETAILING A 'J27' AS NYMR 65894

① The Oxford Rail 'J27' provides an ideal starting point for detailing, although the processes, materials and skills required can be made in advanced to suit how far a modeller wishes to modify the locomotive. The key areas for improvement are replacing the smokebox door, chimney, and dome. Furthermore, scratch building from brass and styrene will also significantly detail the model.

② As with many detailing projects, handling and working on a model is made far more straightforward when disassembled, especially with more comprehensive detailing, as featured here. The ability to easily replace main components on the 'J27s' boiler is trouble-free thanks to the die cast running plate being attached to the plastic boiler with only two screws, this disassembly also helping access for cab detailing later in the process.

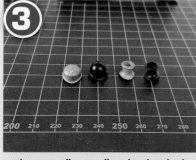

③ The Dave Bradwell 'J27' kit provides detailing castings for both tall (saturated) and lower BR pattern domes, where the latter is required for 65894 and the shape difference compared to Oxford's taller type is particularly noticeable. I also exchanged the factory installed chimney for a casting with more accurate proportions. The castings were all very well rendered, and only required minimal sanding with 1000 grade emery files to remove moulding seams.

④ The moulded smokebox door is the most noticeable drawback with the Oxford 'J27', being undersized and too flat in profile compared to the prototype; replacing the smokebox door with a Dave Bradwell White metal one provides the most significant improvement to the look of any Oxford J27. To centrally fit the new smokebox door, the original door handle was removed and provided a central point to be drilled out: this being required as the White metal door features a rear fixing casting to locate the door centrally.

Preserved 'J27' 0-6-0 65894, as depicted in this modelling guide, stands with a mixed rake of Gresley, Thompson and BR Mk 1 carriages at Grosmont on the North Yorkshire Moors Railway on October 4 2021. Declan Hargreaves

SKILL LEVEL Beginner — Intermediate — Advanced

5

To allow for the new smokebox door to sit flush with the smokebox, a Dremel was used with sanding attachments to gradually flatten the area, this being finished with fine grade emery files. Accommodating the accurately larger door leads to the curved upper handrail needing to be moved upwards by 0.5mm, with the old locating holes being filled with Deluxe Materials plastic putty. At this stage I also replaced the lower smokebox steps with brass strip, as the originals lacked relief.

A smaller feature of 65894 I wanted to replicate are the joining seams along the cabsides and along the firebox cladding. As the Oxford cab and boiler are moulded in plastic, careful scribing of the seams is achieved using a scalpel and steel rule, used very carefully to avoid also scribe through the boiler bands.

6

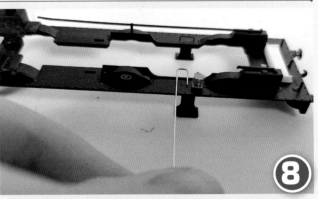

7

The original smokebox door straps on the White metal casting were of the shorter pattern for NER doors, which for 65894 required longer door straps being cut from 0.25mm styrene. The smokebox door number plate was added using a reversed Fox Transfers etched BR numberplate. As 65894 was fitted with vacuum brakes during its first overhaul in preservation, the required vacuum ejector pipe along the boiler was formed from 1mm brass rod.

8

A detail omitted by Oxford Rail on the 'J27' are the mechanical lubricators, with the factory handrails above the side steps fouling directly installing new castings; the small handrails were therefore removed and new cast mechanical lubricators (available from the likes of Markits) installed. New side grab rails were formed by bending 0.5mm brass wire around a handrail bending jig, however, slowly drilling new 0.6mm holes in the die cast running plate is necessary to preserve drill bits!

»

STEP BY STEP **DETAILING A 'J27' AS NYMR 65894**

Out of the box, the 'J27' is modelled with the more common curved cover to the cylinders, however, 65894 features a squared variety. To replicate this, the original cover was cut from the smokebox and the new cover was constructed from layers of 1.0 and 1.5mm square rod section fixed to the running plate for a flush alignment. Also visible is a representation of the mechanical lubricator lines along the front splasher, fabricated from 0.4mm brass wire.

In order to provide more stability while the cab windows were reshaped, the plastic shell was temporarily reunited with the running plate. The cab windows were opened out to remove the old beading with files, before reshaping the top profile of the window with curved files and finally adding new beading from 0.25mm styrene. I also took the opportunity to cut out the moulded cab roof vent and add a plausible cover from thin styrene section.

Clear plastic packaging was cut to form new glazing, with a front 'fixed' window that was cut to the profile of the beading, while the rear sliding window was cut in full relief and glued inside the cab. The wooden frame was painted with a 000 sized brush in a Humbrol metallic copper, replicating varnished wood. Also visible are the rows of fixing rivets along the firebox jacket split line, this being replicated by applying dots of cyano with a cocktail stick.

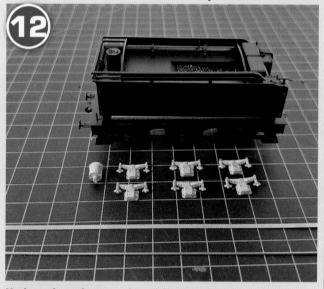

Moving to the tender, more substantial improvements were necessary and can be applied to any Oxford J27. While new axel boxes were castings, fabricating new coal rails and brake rigging forms the more advanced element of the project, using 1.5mm x 0.5mm half round brass rod, requiring a soldered construction for durability, where glue might prove brittle and not allow minute repositioning.

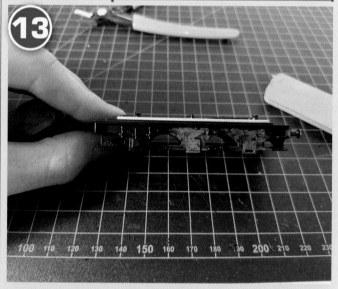

Moulded into the tender chassis, the axel boxes lack relief and replacement with finer castings improves the appearance of the tender. As with the smokebox, a Dremel with burring and sanding attachments gradually cut the axel boxes way before final sanding with 600 and 1000 grit emery sticks. I also added the barely visible slots under each axel box by drilling 0.3mm holes in a pin vice, before opening them up with a scalpel.

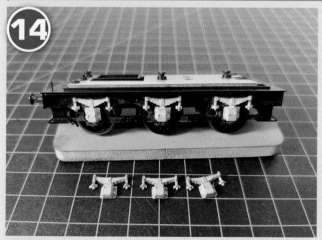

Multiple patterns of axel boxes are supplied with the Dave Bradwell castings and the type most suitable for 65894 already featured finely rendered spring hangars. As with the smokebox, the castings were very clean and required minimal cleaning up of edges with a scalpel before being attached square with cyano.

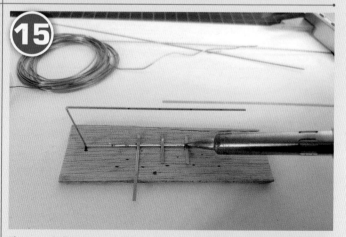

The most challenging part of the project was building new coal rails, as 65894 carries a three-rail variety rather than the two-rail type supplied by Oxford. 1.5mm x 0.5mm half round brass rod was used for the rails themselves and 1.5 x 0.15mm phosphor brass flat section for the supporting brackets. I found it easiest tinning both surfaces with solder before positioning and bonding both with the soldering iron.

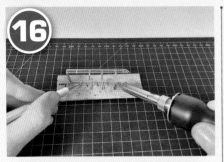

Thirteen supporting brackets were soldered at accurate spacing, firstly only along the lowest coal rail. The other two upper coal rails were each added in turn and carefully soldered, ensuring all three rails remained level and of an even spacing. I found that at least three hands are needed for this process, and I would recommend building a custom jig to hold the brass upright and maintain an even spacing, as I will be sure to do for my second 'J27'!

As Oxford Rail only featured internal brake rigging, a representation of the outer brake rods was required. To allow for easiest access to the tender and pickups, I elected to solder 0.8mm x 0.15mm brass strip to uprights attached to the rear side of the tender frame and in line with the brake shoes: the brass outer rigging was therefore kept separate from the plastic inner rigging, which was retained.

The smokebox, running plate and chassis was brush painted using various mixes of Railmatch roof dirt, matt, and satin black acrylic paints; for a contrast and preservation condition finish, the main black paintwork is the factory finish after an hour of polishing with white spirit and cotton buds, working in a well-ventilated area is a must! All fine-gauge pipework was picked out with varying mixes of Humbrol metallic paints.

The cab detail offered straight from the box is a good starting point, however, it can be significantly improved with further painting and detail. The cab roof was painted in a dark brown to reflect varnished wood before being weathered with black washes, while the cabsides were painted light cream. Additional details included further pipework, new tip down drivers' seat and window runners, all scratch built from brass and styrene, respectively.

Awaiting transfers, the fully painted tender shows the advantage of brass coal rails, offering a more durable and finer appearance than the commonplace moulded plastic rails. The fire irons are included with the 'J27' and are very nicely detailed by Oxford and look perfect once painted a burned brown rust. The lamps are Modelu3D printed LNER style, with one painted BR white and two North Eastern red, as occasionally carried by 65894.

With all final detailed painting completed, including brass beading behind the smokebox and red coupling rods, packs of transfers from Fox and Railtec will complete the model. As I plan loco projects well in advance, I purchase multiple custom Railtec 3D shed plates with an order and as 65894 has carried both 52G and 50A shed plates since 2019, future changes of shed code on my model are possible.

Many preserved locomotives in BR liveries wear cream coloured cabside numbering. However, 65894 is one which features a lighter off-white shade of numbering; to replicate this detail, I used the 10-inch off-white numbering available from Fox Transfers (FRH4008) and when cut close to the backing film, always appear crisp and realistic.

The result of all this hard work is a considerable improvement on the original and proves what can be achieved by a lot of fiddly work and even more patience!

Tools for the JOB

Using a *Hornby Magazine*/Dapol Stove R model as a demonstration piece, **TIM SHACKLETON** takes advantage of years of experience to show how the right tools make kit-building so much easier.

Even the best ready-to-run models are capable of improvement, but all too often a lack of basic skills deters people from attempting any kind of upgrade, even when it's obvious where the issues lie.

In this feature I want to show how you can significantly enhance both the looks and the running qualities of the *Hornby Magazine/Dapol* LMS Stove R, a model that filled a gap in the market when it first appeared in 2009, but which also left room for improvement in the underframe.

The key to all this is knowing how to use the right tools. In the September 2018 issue of *Hornby Magazine,* I outlined the principles involved in the soldered construction of a 4mm scale kit for a BR Palbrick wagon. This present article doubles as a refresher, using as a case study Ian Macdonald's replacement chassis kit

for the Stove R. As with the previous piece, it's not a step-by-step guide so much as an exercise in familiarisation, an informal demonstration of the key stages. By covering what, to my way of thinking, are the most significant elements and not hiding anything important, my hope is that you'll come to realise the process of etched kit construction is a lot simpler – and far less intimidating – than you might have been led to believe.

To many people, however, building etched kits means buying lots of expensive tools, but this just isn't so – I reckon everything I used here, bought new, would set you back little more than half the price of a typical DCC-ready 'OO' gauge locomotive. But think twice about using an old-school etched kit as an apprentice piece, especially something covered in tarnish that came from a swapmeet, or that you've had in a drawer for decades.

I've been building etched kits for a long time now and, thanks to CAD and photo-etch technology, today's sophisticated products are infinitely more accurate, better detailed and above all easier to build than the crude, over-simplified, hand-drawn efforts on which I cut my kit-building teeth.

As with learning any craft skill, the actual work is by no means difficult, but you have to put the hours in and accept that you may not always get things right first time. Take things slowly, learn from your mistakes and sooner than you think you'll be wondering why soldering was absent for so long from your skill set. ∎

Below: **Fairburn 2-6-4T No 42141 is shunting vans between Platform 3 and the through roads at Huddersfield on a summer evening after dark in 1967. The first vehicle is six-wheeled Stove R M32982M which is joined by an ex-Southern Railway PMV.** Tim Shackleton

STEP BY STEP **ENHANCING A STOVE R WITH AN ETCHED CHASSIS KIT**

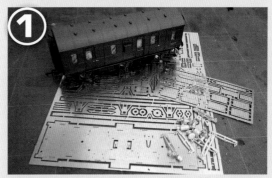

The chassis isn't the strongest point of the *Hornby Magazine*/*Dapol* LMS Stove R, but Ian Macdonald's finescale replacement makes the best of the excellent bodywork. As with all etched kits, assembly skills are required!

Written with the inexperienced builder very much in mind, the kit instructions guide you expertly through the process. The suggested first stage is to emboss rivets on the running gear. Here I'm using a proper riveting tool – if you don't have access to one, these tiny details can just as easily be omitted.

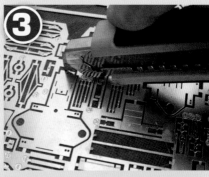

Etched components are held in place on the fret by little tags , but be careful not to confuse them with details. For cutting through them a sharp, heavy blade is essential, while a cutting mat makes the ideal worktop.

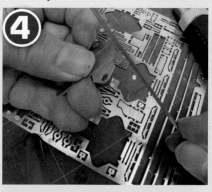

Where parts are detached from the fret small remnants of the tags will probably remain and these can be carefully filed away. I use a No 2 cut flat needle file for this work.

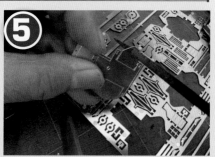

Kits can be under-etched (deliberately or otherwise) and occasionally you may need to enlarge slots and holes slightly, as here where the round brass bearings need to fit snugly into their locating holes. The 'proper' tool to use is a five-sided tapered reamer or cutting broach, but a triangular file will do the job. If you use a round or rat-tailed file, you run the risk of drifting the hole out of alignment or making it oval.

Models are three-dimensional, but etched kits come as flat packs. How do you form the components to shape? The best solution is to use a Hold & Fold, which will give you much more precise control than smooth-jawed pliers. Never ever try and bend parts in your hands.

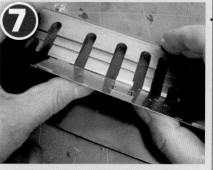

The floor is the largest single component in the kit, containing locating tabs for the bodyshell. With the part trapped tightly along the fold line in the jaws of the Hold & Fold, you can use your thumbs to gently lever up the tabs at right angles.

The outcome. As well as the nine individual jaws – designs vary – you can also use the long continuous edge of the Hold & Fold as a working tool.

Typical toolkit for soldering etched kits – much the same as the one I used in the Palbrick article back in 2018, in fact. I've used Antex 25w soldering irons for years – they're supremely reliable and they cost no more than a ready-to-run wagon. The best work surface for soldering, I find, is a sheet of tufnol, a heat-resistant thermoplastic material used in the electronics industry. An off cut the size of a postcard is enough for most jobs.

For reasons I've never fully understood, soldering terrifies many modellers, but it's one of the simplest of all modelling skills to acquire. Much depends on your choice of solder and the flux you use with it. There's no one-size-fits-all combination but Powerflow has been around for a good few years and does the job well.

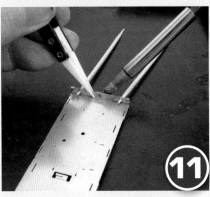

Most etched kits are two-layer affairs – a plain basic shape devoid of detail, and an overlay where half-etching is used to create lines of rivets and other features. The design of etched kits is a sophisticated process but aligning parts can be refreshingly simple. Here I'm using wooden cocktail sticks to hold the buffer-beam overlay in position while I wield the soldering iron. With my other hand I'm using ceramic-tipped tweezers to hold the parts together.

While you let the iron heat up – be patient – add a dab of flux to the area to be soldered and then touch the tip of the iron to the end of your coil of solder. Immediately carry this across to the workpiece and let the iron come into contact with the larger of the two areas to be soldered (this bit is important). Within seconds, solder will flow into the gap between the parts and join them together. While the solder is bright silver, withdraw the iron and use ceramic tipped tweezers (or a lolly stick!) to hold the parts in alignment – ten seconds should be enough.

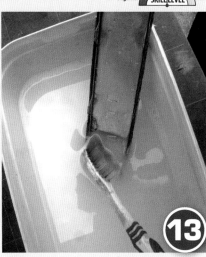

The fluxes used in soldering are highly corrosive and should be scrubbed away immediately the session is over. You'll need to do this at every stage of the assembly process, otherwise stubborn deposits will build up.

Moving along, this is the working part of the chassis, again formed to shape in the Hold & Fold and then soldered for strength. The principle of articulation is amazingly simple – the centre unit slides to and fro across the chassis while the two outer wheelsets pivot, enabling a six-wheel vehicle to negotiate tighter-than-scale curves. I used Alan Gibson 14mm diameter coach wheels rather than the undersized 12mm wheels with which the Stove R came fitted.

With the basic chassis in primer, I've now added the etched brass battery boxes (fold-up numbers that practically clip together) and cast whitemetal details such as buffers, springs and axleboxes. These last can be glued in place with cyano.

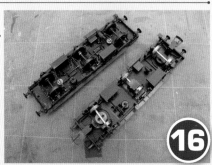

Spot the difference! The kit-built scale chassis has an altogether finer appearance that's especially obvious from underneath. It runs well too; the wheels are a scale 3ft 7ins as per prototype (the RTR model uses 3ft diameter wagon wheels) and the underfloor fitting are a scale size and shape. The scrappy paintwork will soon disappear under a coat of weathering.

The chassis is completely new, but the excellent Dapol body moulding is unmodified. A thin coat of acrylic weathering serves to hide the prismatic effect of the glazing. The bodyshell depicts the Dia. 1796 vans of 1932, which had horizontal beading above and below the windows – a total of 75 were built. Of the Dia 2000 vehicle (45 built 1938-40), many lacked the beading strips or had them removed at some stage. Both types were largely restricted to parcels train service from 1959 onward, following a ban on the use of six-wheeled vehicles in passenger trains. A fair few Stove Rs, carrying a variety of liveries, were still in use when steam finished in 1968 and some subsequently entered departmental service – in the 1970s one even found use as a tool van with the Tinsley breakdown train unit.

COME THE HOUR

As midnight approached, main-line railway stations would come alive with parcels and mail services. Much of it would originate locally, but at many points traffic would be exchanged between trains traveling in different directions. Tim Shackleton's camera captures the excitement of the occasion at Huddersfield in the late summer of 1967, when both eastbound and westbound platforms are piled high with outgoing mail.

At Platform 3, westbound traffic is being handled by a short parcels train that has arrived from the Leeds direction behind Fairburn 2-6-4T

No 42141, which is shunting vans between Platform 3 and the through roads. Other vehicles in the formation include a Mk 1 BG in the then-new blue and grey livery and a Southern utility van. Some of the packages and mailbags that have accumulated on the platform will be awaiting transfer to the following 'Swansea mail' for Stockport, Crewe, Hereford, and Cardiff, interconnecting along the way with other long-distance services tied in with postal distribution.

Half an hour later the Fairburn is still awaiting departure as Stanier 2-6-4T No 42616 brings in the three-coach Huddersfield and Halifax

portion of the evening express from King's Cross, which has been detached at Wakefield. While the engine runs round its train, mail sacks are quickly unloaded from the guard's compartment, ready to be taken by barrow down the subway to the waiting GPO vans standing in the station forecourt. Soon both platforms will have been cleared, ready for the arrival in Platform 3 of the 'Swansea', with its long nightly consist of parcels vans and passenger coaches, as often as not double-headed with Type 4 diesels (and sometimes a steam-diesel combination) for the stiff climb to Standedge.

DIESEL DEPOT
DAWN

While the story of the development of British Railways' fleet of early diesels is often written about, less well known is the detail of how maintenance staff coped with this new form of traction. **EVAN GREEN-HUGHES** looks at the changes made to depots and servicing facilities in the early modernisation era.

Early diesels had to take residence in former steam facilities, as illustrated at Saltley roundhouse on March 24 1967. From left Class 47s D1630 and D1730 share space with Class 25s D5266, D7518, D5288, D1586 and Class 47 D1689 around the turntable. John Chalcraft/Railphotoprints.uk

Although diesel traction was by no means brand new in the years following nationalisation, it only played a minor part in the workings of the UK's railways at that time. Diesel shunting locomotives had been around for almost 20 years and petrol and later diesel railcars had been around for almost half a century. However, these traction units very much played second fiddle to the vast array of steam locomotives that predominated on all but the Southern Region, where third-rail electric power was widespread.

Steam engines were largely housed and maintained in sheds specially designed for the purpose, but which were by the 1950s mostly extremely old and run down. Each location required pits where arriving locomotives could drop their fire and where the old ash would be cleaned out of the firebox and the smokebox. Predominant would be the coaling stage, where fresh coal would be tipped into the tender or engine bunker ready for the next turn of duty, while at larger sheds there might instead be a huge concrete tower for the purpose. Watering

Barely a month old when this image of Brush Type 2 (Class 31) D5593 was taken at Hornsey shed in March 1960, the depot was shared with steam. Not long afterwards the Type 2 was reallocated to the newly built Finsbury Park. To the right of the Type 2 are a pair of BRCW Type 2s, led by D5303, that were initially based at Hornsey but a month later they were transferred to the Scottish region. Norman Preedy/Railphotoprints.uk

facilities would also be provided, usually on a different siding.

All these features generated dirt and dust and this permeated all aspects of the site, including inside the buildings, which were often of the 'roundhouse' pattern in which engines were stabled around a turntable, allowing them to be easily turned before their next duty but also meaning that it was easier to access individual engines, irrespective of the order in which they came on shed.

Because of their relative simplicity, steam locomotives were quite tolerant of this environment and fitting staff were able to conduct the repairs that they needed to do without having to worry too much about contamination from dirt. In any case many of the moving parts could easily be removed and taken into a machine shop when they required attention, while bearings, for instance for coupling rods, could be white metalled off the locomotive and then put back when they had been finished off by hand.

Diesel problems

The arrival of the diesel shunter and the early railcar had not made any impression on these arrangements, in the case of the railcar this was due to the very small number of vehicles involved, while the situation with shunters was a little more complex. Unlike their steam counterparts, diesel shunters could remain at work for 24 hours a day, seven days a week as they did not need to return to depot for coal and water or for cleaning out.

Consequently, many diesel shunters only returned to their home shed when they needed fuel, and for this it was a relatively simple job to equip the steam shed with some sort of bulk fuel facility, although it wasn't unknown for fuel to be distributed directly from rail wagons, and even from road tankers in some places. When on shed the shunters could be accommodated alongside the steam engines without difficulty, and they would be stabled when required much as the tank engines that they had replaced would have been. »

RAILWAY REALISM

British Thompson & Houston Type 1s (Class 15s) 8200 and 8225 stand at the refuelling point at Stratford Depot, probably in the late 1960s or early 1970s. 8200 retains green livery but with full yellow ends, and also the 'D' prefix has been abandoned. *Railphotoprints.uk*

consideration and at first the maintenance of the diesel fleet was not even widely considered.

Although there were by then one or two main line diesels, the country's first foray into mass dieselisation came with the introduction of diesel railcars, now better known as Diesel Multiple Units (DMUs) in 1954. A pilot scheme was decided upon that would see a number of units allocated to the West Riding of Yorkshire where they would be used on an intensive diagram between Leeds, Bradford, and Harrogate. These units would be equipped with underfloor AEC engines, similar to those then in use on London buses, and would have all of their other working parts, including much of the electrical system, fitted below the solebar. Unlike with previous trains there would be no separate locomotive and carriages.

These brand-new aluminium state-of-the-art trains were, without much forethought, allocated to the former Great Northern Railway steam shed at Bowling in Bradford which was, like many steam sheds in the area, a long multi-track dead-end building designed to house large tank engines. As with many steam sheds the yard area was covered in discarded ash, which blew around whenever the weather was dry, and which formed a sticky mulch when it was not. Matters were made worse in that the inside of the building had formerly been whitewashed, but that practice had ceased many years before with the result that the remnants of this covering were peeling off the walls.

Immediately there were problems as the new trains ingested dirt into their workings, making them unreliable, while the new high-quality

This all worked well until the diesel shunters needed any form of maintenance, but in the early years very few repairs were actually conducted at depot level, with anything more than an oil top up usually involving the removal of the coupling rods and a tow back to one or other of the specialist facilities. Of course, work to the rods and much of what was below the frames was very similar to what was done on a steam engine and so was within the capabilities of steam-trained fitting staff. Where repairs were carried out on depot, however, it soon became apparent that the soot, dust, and ash prevalent in the atmosphere presented a hostile environment for diesel traction and resulted in high wear to mechanical components and the total failure of electrical ones.

Some efforts were made to provide facilities for diesel shunter maintenance and one or two depots had separate sections of the shed where this was conducted, but no serious attempt had been made to solve the issue by the time that full dieselisation was under

As more diesels arrive dedicated depots suitable for the new form of traction were built including Stratford Depot in East London. On October 9 1970 Class 47s 1640 and 1535 are joined by Class 46 156 and Class 15 8204 while in the shed are further Class 47s and an early Class 31. *John Medley/Railphotoprints.uk*

interiors were trashed as steam-era men clomped through them treading ash all over the new lino. Needless to say, availability of the new trains was extremely poor, despite the provision of a couple of small rooms being made available for the servicing of individual components removed from the trains themselves.

This mistake was repeated further north when the second batch of similar trains was delivered, with these being allocated to steam sheds in Carlisle and Workington. Additional batches that arrived in Lincolnshire and East Anglia also suffered from the same problems.

New facilities

By 1956 thinking had changed and when it was proposed to introduce DMUs into the Birmingham area the British Railways Board proposed spending £18,800 on the provision of purpose-built facilities at the Monument Lane Carriage sidings in the Ladywood area of the city. This would for the separate diesels from their steam counterparts for the first time.

There storage tanks were provided for diesel fuel, deep pits made for maintenance of all the equipment below the solebar, and a proper six-road shed provided for stabling some of the units. The depot also contained clean rooms that could be used for overhaul of items such as fuel pumps, which relied on absolute cleanliness. The realisation that the new diesel units had more in common with carriages than steam engines had a remarkable effect on availability.

It took something like ten years before most diesel multiple units were being used from purpose-built or adapted facilities, but improvements were made as steam traction

Laira Diesel depot in Plymouth was built specifically for maintenance of the Western Region hydraulic fleet. On October 20 1970 from left to right are Class 43 Warship 855 *Triumph*, Class 52 1021 *Western Cavalier*, Class 43 Warship 838 *Rapid*, and Class 52 1010 *Western Campaigner*. Laira was a good example of a new heavy maintenance depot built from scratch, with no soot, dust, and other steam elements to contaminate the new diesels. John Medley/Railphotoprints.uk

was moved away, for instance the infamous Bradford Hammerton Street depot received a carriage washing machine and had some of its building reconstructed for their new purpose.

At Leith Central depot in Scotland, which had received the Edinburgh-Glasgow units, the main floor level was reduced and on it was placed raised rails, with this modification enabling fitters to work on mechanical components at eye level. Other sheds that were to become synonymous with first generation DMUs, such as South Gosforth in Newcastle, had a massive clean-up but retained their original structures and pit arrangements. Some facilities, such as that at Leeds Neville Hill were eventually rebuilt with new buildings to accommodate the new units.

Larger engines

The 1955 Modernisation Plan proposed the wholesale elimination of steam by diesels, but as these new engines were delivered problems of a similar nature to those that had bedevilled the railcars began to become apparent. Reliability was badly affected by the dirt that these locos were picking up, not only while on depot, but also while they were being used in a generally filthy railway environment. The problem here was that diesels were often being used turn and turnabout with steam locos and were allocated to the same depots, despite those depots having little in the way of specialist facilities for them.

It took a couple of years before the first purpose-built diesel depot was made available, with this being built at Stratford in East London on part of the site of the existing steam depot, which was one of the largest in the country and at one time had more than 300 locomotives based there.

Stratford A shed opened in 1958 and was to a revolutionary design which saw a large four-road shed built that had both pits and also platform level walkways that enabled fitters to easily get to all the working parts of the new diesels. Specialist lifting and handling equipment was also installed, while outside there were a number of sidings that could be used to stable diesels when they were not in use. These were completely separate to those used by the depots steam traction. Refuelling facilities were also enhanced, with pumps being provided in between the depot tracks, with each having an awning over it, while the actual bulk fuel storage was some distance away.

Two years later a new depot opened at Finsbury Park, north of King's Cross station, and this was the first purpose-built facility designed to cope with main line diesel locos, varying from previous depots in that it was not a conversion of a steam depot but was instead built from scratch on a new site. This depot had six under cover maintenance roads which contained three-level full-length inspection facilities as well as sunken tracks. Glass was extensively used both at the front of the building above the doors and in the roof so as to give a light and airy feeling and there were roller shutter doors at the end of each road, although these seem to have been rarely used. »

RAILWAY REALISM

The depot also contained the latest equipment for handling heavy parts, thus reducing the physical effort required of the staff, but also making the depot a safer place in which to work. Outside there were five roads within and another five roads outside for stabling engines, as well as fuelling facilities. This shed played host to most of the East Coast Main line's top-link motive power after the demise of steam, including the famous Deltics, but also the less-glamorous engines that were used on the intensive suburban services in that area, including Class 26s, Class 31s, and the somewhat unsuccessful Baby Deltics. The arrangement of the platforms inside the maintenance building was particularly successful for maintaining English Electric Type 1s, or Class 20s, where work had to be carried out from the outside due to the lack of a totally enclosed body.

Most of the regions received at least one of the new major diesel depots, with in most cases these replacing a larger number of former sheds. One of the most famous was to be Eastfield, which was situated at the end of the tunnel and Cowlairs bank leading from Glasgow Queen Street station, and which was to supply all the motive power for the West Highland lines. It was a huge concrete structure with the main shed having seven roads all provided on the site of some of the former steam facilities. This shed had actually been in working since 1904 but the removal of steam by 1966 allowed diesel facilities to be extended until the depot had six through maintenance roads as well as four single-ended roads and a separate wheel lathe shop. Like many diesel depots a large office block was also provided. Although the depot closed in 1992 following the replacement of loco working by multiple units, it is interesting to note that it reopened in 2004 following an investment of £14m, allowing for construction of a much-reduced facility for the servicing of DMUs.

Improved maintenance

The arrival of purpose-built depots also saw a step change in the way that locos were maintained, with the end of the steam-era principle of only repairing something when it was broken and the adoption of a routine that would typically see a loco working a five-day roster, following which it would return to its home depot for a check and scheduled maintenance. This style of maintenance saw British Railways aim for a typical express loco to be covering in the order of 4,200 miles a week to meet its financial targets.

Despite the amount of money that was invested in the modernisation programme it proved impossible to provide such purpose-built facilities in every region, and as a result some ingenious ways were found to accommodate the new traction. A typical example was Leeds Holbeck Depot, which was home to a large number of diesels that worked services over the Settle-Carlisle, to Hull and cross-country routes to Birmingham as well as the large number of local freight workings running in the area. The depot had a couple of large roundhouses that were not really suitable for the new diesels and so early in the early 1960s the former machine shops, which were long buildings accessed from only one end were converted for the examination, service, and repair of diesels, which eventually numbered more than 100. A new fuelling point was added outside, although this suffered from being placed fairly near to a giant steam-age coaling tower, while most of the adjacent storage roads were assigned diesel only. This arrangement lasted for several years as the depot did not say goodbye to steam engines until as late as September 1967, after which the coaling tower was demolished along with the roundhouses with the subsequent space being used for further open-air storage for diesels.

There was a slightly different quandary at Thornaby on Teesside because there a brand-new depot had been constructed in 1957, which

Central headcode Class 40 40163 heads a line of Class 40s and a Class 25 awaiting attention inside Reddish Depot on June 3, 1979. *Railphotoprints.uk*

replaced four smaller facilities, but this depot had been designed specifically to cater for steam engines. It comprised of a roundhouse 300ft in diameter that contained 22 stabling roads and a 70ft long turntable, a running shed with facilities for preparing locomotives under cover and also the damping down of ash as it was removed from fireboxes and smokeboxes. There was a huge coaling plant that could hold 390 tons of coal and 15 watering points that were supplied by a water tank containing 200,000 gallons of water. Also provided were facilities for maintenance and repair.

Costing £1.25m the shed was entirely constructed of reinforced concrete. Quite why so much money was spent on providing facilities for steam engines some two years after the modernisation plan was announced is something of a mystery and in the event much of what was spent was wasted because the shed was only to survive in its original form for seven years, by which time the last steam engines had been withdrawn from the area. Apparently, the original plan had been to include two roundhouses, but during a review one was dropped, due to the impending arrival of the diesels. Presumably, no one thought that the steam engine would be eliminated so quickly.

Diesel conquest

Thornaby had in fact had diesels almost from its opening and it received a large number of Class 25s and 37s in the early 1960s. These had to be stored and serviced alongside the steam engines in the new shed, but the elimination of steam allowed the long single-ended sheds to be repurposed for diesels, although in this case the depot was not fitted with triple-height inspection platforms and instead relied on its steam-style inspection pits, which remained in use until the depot was finally taken out of service in the early 1980s.

The roundhouse served as a store and was increasingly used to accommodate wagons before it was inevitably knocked down, no doubt many years before it was worn out. Changing patterns of freight traffic and the almost universal use of multiple units for passenger work meant that the depot's importance swiftly declined until it only housed withdrawn engines and a few shunters. Today the site has been cleared.

In the 1960s the Beeching plan led to the building of several massive new hump marshalling yards, which were usually situated on green field sites not previously used for railway facilities. This meant that **»**

The steam era coaling stage stood for many years after being made redundant. In this image dated May 11 1985 Class 37 37069 is joined by Class 47s 47299, 47295, 47105, 47358 and 47222. *Gordon Edgar/Railphotoprints.uk*

many of the old locomotive depots were now no longer conveniently sited for the work that was being done. For instance the new marshalling yard at Healey Mills, on the Calder Valley line near Ossett, West Yorkshire, was provided with traction from depots in Leeds, Wakefield and Mirfield, and this led to a great deal of wasteful mileage, so much so that in the 1960s it was common to see lines of engines queued up at stations such as Wakefield Kirkgate awaiting entry into the steam shed, having made the journey from Healey Mills light engine.

In time this wasteful practice led to many marshalling yards having small diesel sheds added, which would contain a relatively small number of engines, but which could be used for general servicing, repair, and refuelling, thus eliminating much light engine mileage. Diesels would then be stabled around the depot area and would be available for duty as and when required. Most of these facilities were small two or three road sheds that could contain only two

Above: **Grangemouth depot plays host to a selection of motive power after an overnight dusting of snow on March 23 1986. Peeking out of the former steam shed (65F) and awaiting their call to duty at the port and elsewhere in the region are Class 20 20138, Class 37s 37058 and 37051, and Class 27 27063.** Gordon Edgar/Railphotoprints.uk

Below: **One of the last turntables to remain in use at a major depot was the one at Old Oak Common. The depot had four of them all undercover in steam days, and this was the only one to survive. Class 50 50035** *Ark Royal* **gingerly move onto the table on May 8 1990.** Railphotoprints.uk

The first of the Class 58s, 58001, stands outside the huge depot at Toton on August 11 1984. The facility was built on the site of the former steam shed to serve the Midlands coal traffic. Today the depot is the centre of activity for DB Cargo and its fleet of Class 60s, 66s and 67s.
Railphotoprints.uk

or three locos per line and were also provided with accommodation blocks for crew use as well as refuelling bays, making them ideal and compact subjects for the railway modeller.

The 1960s also saw a move away from the provision of general facilities for the storage and maintenance of traction units and a move towards specialisation. The Western Region was one of two that received examples of the revolutionary Blue Pullman multiple units that came into traffic in 1957 and ran from London Paddington to Bristol, Cardiff, and Birmingham. These were the first to use diesel power cars at each end of a train of coaches and as such remained in fixed formation. Existing depot facilities were almost all designed to deal with individual traction units, while DMU depots were mainly set out to deal with trains fitted with underfloor traction equipment, so alternative arrangements had to be made. One depot that was converted for this use was Bristol Barton Hill, which had opened in 1840 as a loco depot but which was later converted to accommodate carriages and wagons. This was taken over for Blue Pullman use and a new two-road shed was built, complimenting the buildings that were already there. This compact shed became a loco depot again in 1995 when it was taken over by Rail Express Systems and it still exists today and is used for the overnight servicing the Voyager units of Cross-Country trains. At Old Oak Common the units were housed in the 'Pullman Shed', a long building ideal for housing such trains.

Step change

The introduction of diesel traction was a step change for the British Railways motive power department. At first it wasn't understood that diesels did not require as much time on shed as steam engines and so the level of facilities provided in the early days merely mirrored that provided for the older form of traction. As more was understood of the workings of the new diesels it became apparent that each would be off shed far longer than its steam counterpart and thus the amount of space required on the depot would be much less than before. More complex maintenance was also moved from depot level to works level, which again meant less space was required for facilities such as machine shops. As things progressed it became apparent that maintenance and thus availability would be improved by giving staff easier access to the working areas of locos, which unlike steam were largely above solebar level, and this led to purpose-built sheds being built with multi-layer working platforms and specialist parts handing equipment. A clean working environment was also established, particularly once steam was done away with, and specialist ultra-clean areas were constructed where components such as fuel systems could be overhauled.

Nowadays there are far fewer diesel depots than there used to be due to the increasing use of diesel multiple units, and many stabling points consist of no more than lines of tracks with walkways in between and from which cleaning and day-to-day checks can be performed. The diesel depot of the 1960s, although regarded as ultra-modern in its time, is now as dated as the steam roundhouse was before it, yet it represents a period in history that is fast becoming one of the most prominent amongst railway modellers and historians. ∎

Biomass for the MASSES

2022 saw the arrival of Accurascale's most modern 'Powering Britain' collection freight wagons – the HYA and IIA fleet. **MIKE WILD** models the latest power station trains by weathering a Hornby GBRf Class 60 and a rake of Accurascale IIA biomass bogie hoppers for 'OO' gauge.

Expansion of the GBRf Class 60 fleet started with acquisition of former Colas Rail Freight locomotives and the first step was removal of the Colas wording from the side. Now operated by GBRf, 60087 Bountiful approaches Whitley Bridge on January 13 2020 heading the 6.24am Tyne Coal Terminal-Drax loaded biomass hoppers. Paul Biggs

Block trains of matching wagons are a hallmark of the modern railway as bulk flows provide an efficient means of moving large quantities of goods across the country. Coal was once one of the biggest traffic volumes on the railways, but the large-scale reduction in coal burning power stations meant the railway had to respond to a new fuel type – biomass.

GBRf and wagon manufacturer WH Davis saw the opportunity to use recently introduced HYA high capacity bogie coal hoppers as the basis for a conversion project and began undertaking modifications to the GBRf HYA fleet – some of which had only been service for three years, the first was delivered in 2007.

WH Davis completed its first biomass wagon conversion in 2009 and eventually completed 200, coded IIA, which would be dedicated to the new traffic type. They had to have pneumatically opening hoods to keep the load protected from the elements, particularly rain, while in trans, with the rail company adding two piece load bay covers to each wagon. These conversions were joined by new build wagons dedicated to biomass traffic while other HYA wagons were modified for denser aggregate traffic by reducing their length.

Much of the GBRf biomass traffic is in the north of England, with flows from Liverpool Docks, Hull, Newcastle and Immingham taking fuel transported by sea to Drax power station, which uses 7.5 million tonnes of biomass each year. Incredibly that amounts to 17 trains per day running six days a week with each train conveying enough biomass to

supply electricity to just over 800 houses for a year. Unloading takes less than 40 minutes for a full train. Around 300,0000 tonnes of biomass is stored on site at Drax with another train-load arriving every 90 minutes to keep Drax generating electricity for the UK.

Accurascale Models

Such a major freight operation is important for modellers. For decades we have modelled coal trains from the steam era and diesel era with formations of 16ton mineral wagons, 21ton hoppers and since the late 1960s the HAA coal hopper family. Accurascale's new collection of wagons for 2022 covered the HYA/IIA fleet in original coal carrying format with open hoppers in GBRf and Fastline liveries as well as the IIA biomass wagons. The latter are the subject of this modelling guide.

The first production run arrived in April 2022 with a choice of four twin packs. Each contained a pair of individually numbered wagons that carry more than 150 separate tampo prints on each side of the wagon – incredibly there are 25 separate prints on each bogie.

Detail matches the prototypes in every respect with sprung buffers at all four corners, small tension lock couplings in NEM pockets, turned metal wheels, hopper bottom detail, handbrake wheels, separate conduits along the body and modelling the hopper covers and mechanism. One pack is also supplied with a factory fitted flashing tail lamp which is switched on with a magnetic sensor at the rear of the wagon, while an accessory pack with each pair includes brake pipes and dummy screw link couplings for optional use.

While these wagon look superb out of the box with their pristine silver finish, the real wagons soon weathered in service, so for this project we decided to model a full biomass train, including a suitable locomotive, to create an authentic formation.

Motive Power

GBRf biomass trains are handled by one of two locomotive types: the Brush built Class 60 Co-Co heavy freight diesel-electrics and its ubiquitous Class 66 fleet. The Class 60s used by GBRf have been seen in de-branded Colas Rail Freight black, orange and yellow as well as the new GBRf blue and orange livery, while Class 66s in a variety of corporate and one-off liveries have been turned out on the trains.

Our choice of motive power for this project is Hornby's model of 60095 in GBRf blue, but we could have chosen Bachmann or Hattons Class 66s in a variety of liveries. Even BR large logo blue liveried 66789 has been seen on biomass trains.

Hornby's model of 60095 is smartly presented in the blue and orange colour scheme of the freight operator, but there were a couple of mis-positioned electrification warning flashes on the model, so before we started the weathering process we removed these carefully with a small amount of Isopropyl Alcohol (IPA). IPA is very good at removing paint, but you have to be very careful not to overdo its use as it will remove all paint if used to vigorously.

The three warning flashes were positioned against the cantrail on one side of the locomotive, all of which were removed and replaced with Fox Transfers water slide »

EXCLUSIVE VIDEO ONLINE!
WWW.KEYMODELWORLD.COM
SEE IT IN ACTION

The lightly weathered Hornby Class 60 looks just the part as it leads the rake of newly weathered Accurascale biomass hoppers.

decals. The removal process leaves a shiny patch behind, but as we are weathering this locomotive that will be covered over later.

Having completed the warning flashes the accessory pack for the Class 60 was opened up and fitted starting with the full valance at the exhaust end and the open valances at the other end so that the NEM coupling socket can be used. The finishing touch before weathering was the addition of the air-brake and main reservoir pipes (red one upper, yellow lower) and the dummy screw link coupling in the centre.

Weathering was a four-colour process on the Class 60, as these locomotives always appear well turned out but do attract typical frame and roof dirt that you would expect from a hard-working engine. The colour selected for 60095 are Lifecolor Frame Dirt (UA719), Burned Black (UA736) and Dirty Black (UA731) plus Tamiya Flat Black (XF-1). The step by step guide explains how we used these colours.

Rolling Stock

The biomass wagons, like the Class 60, look superb in pristine condition, but for a realistic in-service train we needed a much more workmanlike appearance with thorough weathering. The only other change we made to these wagons was replacement of the couplings with West Hill Wagon Works supplied Hunts magnetic couplings for easy connection of the train.

Beyond the coupling change it is all about the weathering. Photographs of these wagons in service show them to be quite monotone in their staining so our choice was to work with

two colours: Lifecolor Burned Black (UA736) as a base colour for the underframe and bogies followed by Dirty Black (UA731) to add further depth to the upper weathering.

This time the process is more involved. The paint application is carried out by airbrush, but it is more about how and how much paint that is taken off. Having airbrushed the underframes, the roof and upper bodysides are flat brush moistened (not doused) in airbrush cleaner, which is then used to draw the paint down the body side to create a streaked effect down the wagon sides to represent rain washing the dirt down the sides. This softens the weathering too and offers a realistic finish that is topped off by a further coat of Dirty Black over the top.

However, you could go further and use weathering specialist TMC which is offering weathered versions with graffiti on the wagon sides. This takes the weathered finish to

another level and the company can carry out the full process to deliver you a brand-new wagon ready weathered to run on your layout. For this guide we had the opportunity to inspect a pair of wagons from TMC with Hornby Magazine graphics added to their sides, but any type of graffiti can be added.

Step by Step

Modelling a full train is a rewarding process, as the result is a complete formation that looks just like the real thing, and the step by step guide explains how we went about changing the warning flashes, adding the details and finally the weathering. There were, though, two finishing touches for this project: the addition of Digitrains ZIMO sound for the Class 60 using a new MS450 chip with an 8-pin plug, plus a Modelu3D printed driver suitably painted to decorate the cab. 60095 is now ready for service.

Visit www.keymodelworld.com/weathering to see our full collection of weathering guides. ∎

WHAT WE USED		
Product	Supplier	Cat No.
Class 60 60095, GBRf blue	www.hornby.com	R30025
IIA biomass bogie hoppers	www.accurascale.com	Various
Modern electrification warning flashes	www.fox-transfers.co.uk	F4214/2
Lifecolor Frame Dirt arylic paint	www.airbrushes.com	UA719
Lifecolor Burned Black acrylic paint	www.airbrushes.com	UA736
Lifecolor Dirty Black acrylic paint	www.airbrushes.com	UA731
Tamiya Flat Black acrylic paint	www.tamiya.com	XF-1

GRAFFITI EFFECTS FROM TMC

Weathering specialist TMC is now offering graffiti paint effects for modern wagons. This pair of Accurascale biomass hopper have received the full treatment, together with Hornby Magazine and Key Model World graffiti. Look closely and you will see who the 'artists' are too! Visit *www.themodelcentre.com* for more information.

GBRf's Class 60 60095 passes Raskelf on the East Coast Main Line with the 06.24 Tyne Coal Terminal to Drax loaded biomass hoppers on May 11 2021. The wagons are heaveily weathered in this view, but 60095 is still in smart condition. Paul Biggs

STEP BY STEP **MODELLING A GBRF BIOMASS TRAIN IN 'OO'**

1 Hornby's model of GBRf Class 60 60095 will head up this biomass train. Its livery is smartly presented, but this side has the electrification warning flashes positioned too high on the bodyside.

2 The three warning flashes on this side sit across the orange bar at the top while images of the locomotive show them positioned at the top of the blue bodyside section. They are simple to remove and replace with waterslide transfers.

3 Using Isopropyl Alcohol (IPA) the original printed warning flashes are carefully removed using a cotton bud moistened with IPA to take off the printing. Work carefully and slowly so that you don't go all the way through the paint.

4 The removal process continues for the other two warning flashes which are positioned above the central engine room doors and next to the other cab door.

5

A sheet of Fox Transfers modern electrification warning flashes is used to replace the original versions. These are dipped in water and the positioned on the model using a small paint brush. Take away the excess water with kitchen paper then leave overnight for the decals to set.

6 While the transfers set the accessory pack for the Class 60 can be added. We only want a coupling at one end of the locomotive, so the full valance was added at the exhaust end of the diesel. We used Roket Rapid superglue to fix it in place.

7 Next the same adhesive is used to fit the air brake pipes and dummy screw link coupling. Note the orientation of the brake and main reservoir pipes – red upper, yellow lower.

Beginner — Intermediate **SKILL LEVEL** — Advanced

8 At the No 2 end the open valance is fitted to allow use of the NEM coupling pocket to connect the Class 60 to its soon to be weathered rake of IIA biomass wagons.

9 Weathering of the Class 60 starts at the underframe with an application of Lifecolor Frame Dirt (UA719). This is applied with an airbrush only to the underframe using a business card as a mask to prevent over spray onto the bodyside. The contrast between fresh black plastic and the Frame Dirt is clear.

10 Continuing along the underframe it is important to move the angle of the airbrush to work around the central parts, which could otherwise be missed. Not the lack of overspray on the body, controlled using a business card as a simple and effective mask.

11 Also important is to ensure that the tops of the bogies are weathered – if these are missed it would stand out when the model negotiated a curve. Turn each bogie to the side to weather these areas with the same Frame Dirt colour.

12 The Class 60 has now been inverted to allow the underside of the bogies and underframe components to be weathered using the same airbrush application method and Frame Dirt colour.

13 The underframe is now complete and 60095 is already looking more realistic. We do want to add a little weathering to the roof, but not too much as these locomotives are kept fairly smart by their operator.

14 The first port of call on the roof is the exhaust. We start with an application of Lifecolor Tensocrom Rust 2 (TSC 206) from an airbrush. The patches will dry and be overlaid by further colours.

15 Burned Black is applied over and around the exhaust next, but not too heavily or it will disguise the previously applied rust colour completely.

16 Further Burned Black is added along the roof from an airbrush as a base layer of roof weathering. As with the underframe and business card was used as a mask to prevent overspray onto the body.

17 The painted applied in Step 16 is now modulated with a flat brush moistened with airbrush cleaner. This allows the flat airbrushed colour to be streaked to represent rain water drawing dirt down the roof.

18 The same process continues around the cab roofs and you can also see how the subtle application of Burned Black on the exhaust allows the rust colour to show through.

STEP BY STEP | **MODELLING A GBRF BIOMASS TRAIN IN 'OO'**

⑲

Further streaking of the Burned Black roof colour takes the paint lightly down the bodyside. Following this another light application of Burned Black was made over the roof to soften the brush strokes and represent fresh dirt build up.

⑳

Finally the Class 60 receives a two colour exhaust stain at one end – Lifecolor Dirty Black (UA731) followed by Tamiy Flat Black (XF-1).

㉑

The full set of wagons extends to ten vehicles, all of which need a similar finish but with slight variations. The method outlined here allows for that. Each wagon starts out in pristine condition as delivered by Accurascale.

㉒

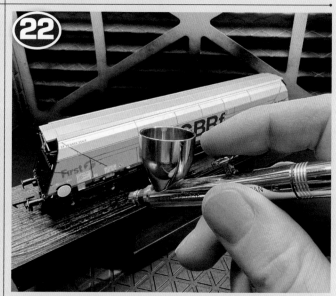

As with the Class 60 an Iwata Eclipse CS dual action airbrush is used for the paint application. This time the colour cup is loaded with Lifecolor Burned Black (UA736) as a base colour for the underframe.

㉓

Having weathered the underframe, the undersides of the loading bay doors were touched in too.

㉔

The same colour is the used to soften the factory solid black of the wagon ends, applied using the same airbrush.

SKILL LEVEL Beginner · Intermediate · Advanced

Inverting the wagon allows the underside to be weathered fully using Burned Black.

Moving to the roof, multiple passes build up the colour on the top of the wagon and while it looks speckled and thin at this point the finished paint will be much more dense.

Further layers of Burned Black have been built up over the roof now increasing the amount of paint on the wagon.

Using a flat brush moistened with airbrush cleaner the newly applied weathering paint can be drawn down the wagon sides to create streaks and stains. This is a time when you can play with the colour to give each wagon a slightly different finish, but within the same colour spectrum.

This wagon is now almost complete, except for a few areas that need a final adjustment of the Burned Black colour with a paint brush.

Completing the look for these wagons is an application of Lifecolor Dirty Black (UA731) from the airbrush to blend the previously applied Burned Black and streaks together, this takes away any hard edges. Nine more wagons to go!

'TT:120' IS HERE!

For the first time in 50 years a new model railway scale has come to the British market. **MIKE WILD** details the launch of 'TT:120' – a scale which is set to make a big splash in the world of model railways.

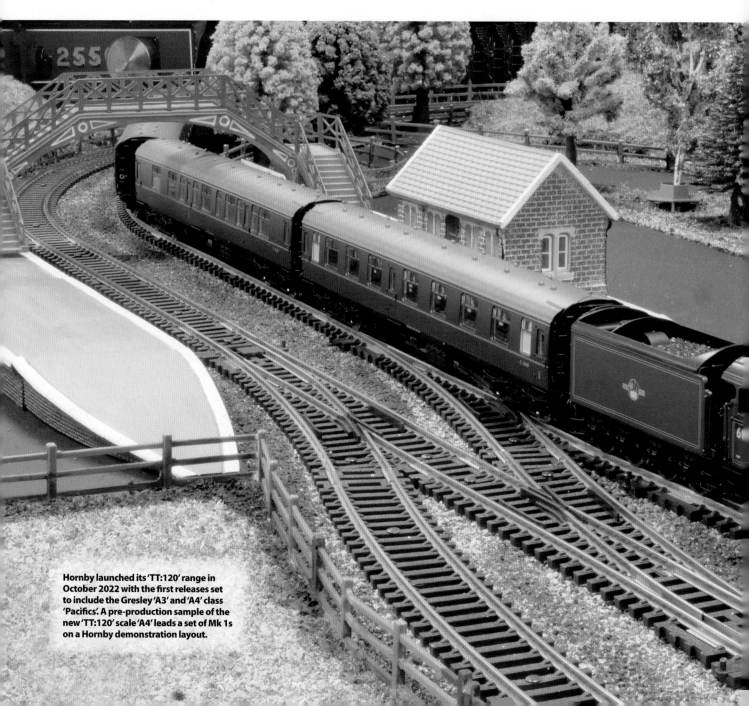

Hornby launched its 'TT:120' range in October 2022 with the first releases set to include the Gresley 'A3' and 'A4' class 'Pacifics'. A pre-production sample of the new 'TT:120' scale 'A4' leads a set of Mk 1s on a Hornby demonstration layout.

This is a one in a lifetime change for railway modelling. The introduction of a brand-new scale is a very rare occasion, but 2022 saw the arrival of just that with the launch of 'TT:120'. The new name in British model railways might seem familiar, as 'TT' (Table Top railways) was part of the Tri-ang range in the 1960s, but it soon faded away to make way for the more popular 'OO' gauge.

The original 'TT' used models made to 3mm:1ft scale (1:100) running on 12mm gauge track. Like the other mainstream British model railway scales of 'OO' and 'N' gauge it wasn't a true scale as the locomotives and rolling stock were made to a larger scale than their track – the latter being under scale. However, this time round 'TT:120' offers a true scale for the entire collection across locomotives, track, buildings and accessories making it stand out from the crowd.

If you are familiar with model railway scales you will already have worked out that the new 'TT:120' is smaller than the most common 'OO' gauge (1:76 scale), but it is also bigger than 'N' gauge (1:148) and provides a handy half-way

Only available at: www.hornby.com/HornbyTT120

Hornby 'TT:120s' mantra is Small World, Big Ideas. This is the cover for the manufacturer's first catalogue for the new school.

size between the two to offer a compromise between space and ease of handling.

The first products to be revealed for 'TT:120' came to light in June when Peco revealed its new collection of track components plus a range of building kits and platform components to allow a layout to be built. However, there was a big hole to be filled for rolling stock, which soon brought announcements from Heljan (since withdrawn) while Gaugemaster instantly saw the potential of the new scale with its European 1:120 scale products that includes figures, buildings, road vehicles and many more accessories. Plus, it also hinted at the idea of bringing a European model of the Class 66 into the British market.

All this was exciting, but what 'TT:120' was lacking was a complete system. We had the possibility of building a layout – scenic materials from existing sources would be perfectly suitable – but we didn't have a complete system or trains which could be run together.

Enter Hornby 'TT:120'

On October 10, 2022 Hornby revealed its brand-new range of 'TT:120' scale model railway products – and it went big. Locomotives (in multiple), carriages, wagons, track, buildings and accessories were all revealed as the grand fanfare for Hornby's first all-new product range in 50 years.

Hornby saw the potential for 'TT:120' to suit modern homes where space is at a premium and had spent more than three years developing its plans for the scale so that it would be able to deliver a broad range of attractive and joined up products to the market soon after the launch.

Hornby's product launch covers a spectrum of items from starter train sets to individual locomotives, carriages and wagons as well as »

USEFUL LINKS	
Hornby **TT:120'**	www.hornby.com/hornbytt120
Peco	www.peco-uk.com
Gaugemaster	www.gaugemaster.com
West Hill Wagon Works	www.westhillwagonworks.co.uk

its own track system, buildings and, through Oxford Diecast, road vehicles.

"We have been developing Hornby TT:120 for several years", explained Simon Kohler, Marketing & Product Development Director at the launch, "and it represents a substantial investment. Hornby TT:120 provides many solutions for those who really want to create a model railway but have little or no space for the larger 'OO' size."

The first components of the new Hornby 'TT:120' collection due to arrive this autumn were track and buildings, but excitingly modellers won't have long to wait for the first trains sets to arrive as they are due into stock before Christmas.

Interestingly, Hornby is also changing its distribution for 'TT:120'. The Margate-based company will be selling its new range exclusively through its dedicated website and has set up a Hornby TT:120 Club with membership benefits including 15% discount on all purchases from the new range.

Hornby's products

The first sets to be produced by Hornby for 'TT:120' will be the 'Easterner' (Cat No. TT1002M) containing Gresley 'A4' 4-6-2 60004 *William Whitelaw* in BR lined green, a trio of BR Mk 1 carriages, an oval of track and a controller. This will be joined by the 'Scotsman' set (TT1001M) which contains Gresley 'A3' 4-6-2 2550 *Blink Bonny* in LNER lined apple green, three Pullman cars with lights and the same circuit of track and controller. Prices are set at £194.49 and £215.99 respectively.

The sets will be joined in the new year by the arrival of three further 'A4s' modelling 4468 *Mallard* in LNER garter blue (TT3007M), 60016 *Silver King* in BR lined green (TT3008M) and 60025 *Falcon* in BR lined blue (TT3009M) plus

Skaledale buildings are coming for 'TT:120' from Hornby. The first will be a collection of railway buildings based on structures at Dent station that have previously been made in 'OO' gauge.

HORNBY 'TT:120' LOCOMOTIVES – PHASE 1-4		
Class	**Status**	**Release phase**
LNER Gresley 'A3' 4-6-2	Production	Phase 1
LNER Gresley 'A4' 4-6-2	Production	Phase 1
LMS Stanier 'Duchess' 4-6-2	3D sample	Phase 2
BR '9F' 2-10-0	CAD drawing	Phase 3
GWR 'Castle' 4-6-0	CAD drawing	Phase 3
BR 'Britannia' 4-6-2	Development	Phase 4
LMS Stanier 'Black Five' 4-6-0	Development	Phase 4
GWR Collett '57XX' 0-6-0PT	Development	Phase 4
Hunslet 'J94' 0-6-0ST	Development	Phase 4
Class 08 0-6-0 diesel shunter	Engineering sample	Phase 1
Class 50 Co-Co diesel electric	3D sample	Phase 2
Class 66 Co-Co diesel electric	3D sample	Phase 2
Class 43 HST power cars	3D sample	Phase 2
Class 31 A1A-A1A diesel electric	Development	Phase 3
Class 37 Co-Co diesel electric	Development	Phase 3
Class 47 Co-Co diesel electric	Development	Phase 3
Class 60 Co-Co diesel electric	Development	Phase 3
Class 67 Bo-Bo diesel electric	Development	Phase 4
Class 73 Bo-Bo electro-diesel	Development	Phase 4
Class 800 bi-mode unit	Development	Phase 4

Hornby's approach to 'TT:120' is to create a complete system covering locomotives, rolling stock, track, trainsets, buildings and accessories. A whole collection of products are in development for steam and diesel era modellers.

match European products. You can also expect die-cast metal chassis, working lights on diesel locomotives, turned metal wheels, metal valve gear, many separately fitted parts, detailed livery application and variations within the class such as 'A4s' with and without valances, 'A3s' without and with German smoke deflectors, different cab doors on the Class 08s and much more.

Hornby's 'TT:120' range extends to rolling stock with the first phase set to deliver individual Pullman Kitchen First and Brake Third coaches together with BR Mk 1 Corridor Composite (CK) and Brake Second Corridor (BSK) vehicles. There will also be a collection of Stanier Period III 57ft corridor coaches, BR Mk 2E locomotive-hauled vehicles and HST Mk 3 trailer coaches. Future development includes plans for Gresley and Collett corridor carriages for LNER and GWR modellers together with BR Mk 1 parcels stock.

Freight vehicles start with seven-plank open wagons, 12ton vent vans and 14ton tank wagons for the steam era and ex-LNER diagram 034 'Toad' brake vans. Modern era modellers will benefit from the HAA Merry-Go-Round hopper as well as the TTA tanker while future releases will cover VEA and VGA vans, KFA container flats and Seacow ballast hoppers.

Like the locomotives, all rolling stock will have NEM coupling pockets and turned metal wheels making them free running on the track.

Track choices

The track gauge for 'TT:120' is 12mm between the rails – the same as the previous 'TT' gauge products of the 1960s, but now the locomotives and rolling stock are to scale rather than being oversize for the track.

The 'TT:120' track range from Hornby will be based around code 80 rail and will focus on sectional track pieces and insulated frog points. The range will cover first-fourth radius curves together with left and right-hand points, »

HORNBY 'TT:120' CARRIAGES AND WAGONS – PHASE 1-4		
Vehicle	**Status**	**Phase**
Pullman carriages	Production	Phase 1
LMS Stanier 57ft Period III coaches	Engineering sample	Phase 1
BR Mk 1 carriages	Production	Phase 1
BR Mk 2E carriages	Engineering sample	Phase 2
BR Mk 3 carriages	Engineering sample	Phase 2
LNER Gresley corridor carriages	Development	Phase 3
GWR Collett bow-end carriages	Development	Phase 4
BR Mk 1 parcels vans	Development	Phase 4
Seven-plank open wagon	Decoration samples	Phase 1
GWR 12ton ventilated van	Decoration samples	Phase 1/2
12ton tanker	Decoration samples	Phase 1/2
LNER 'Toad' brake van	Decoration samples	Phase 1/2
BR 21-ton mineral wagon	Engineering samples	Phase 1/2
BR HAA coal hopper	Engineering samples	Phase 1/2
BR TTA tanker	Engineering samples	Phase 1/2
BR Conflat wagon	Development	Phase 3/4
BR Mk 1 horsebox	Development	Phase 3/4
BR VEA box van	Development	Phase 3/4
KFA container flat	Development	Phase 3/4
YGB seacow ballast wagon	Development	Phase 3/4
VGA box van	Development	Phase 3/4

The Class 08 shunter is set to become Hornby's first diesel locomotive release for 'TT:120'.

crossings and power tracks to begin with further plans for expansion in the future.

All track components will be available individually and customers will also be able to choose from a selection of track extension packs to expand an initial 'TT:120' train set. As with the Hornby 'OO' gauge sectional track, rail joiners will be pre-fitted to all track components making them simple to join together to create a layout plan.

A basic second radius circuit with a siding outside the circuit, as supplied in the train sets, requires just 1,250mm x 840mm – a little over 4ft in length and just under 2ft 6in. A third radius circuit will need 706mm in width, fourth radius 792mm, while the largest available is a

sixth radius curve which will need 1,280mm to complete a full return curve. Hornby's first points are crossings are offer a 15-degree angle with options for left- and right-hand points plus left and right-handed crossings.

Hornby's track system is all based around code 80 profile rail (0.080in tall flat bottom rail) set into plastic sleepers, but there is a second and finer choice in Peco's new 'TT:120' track range.

The Peco range is all made with code 55 rail (0.055in tall flat bottom rail) which is the same as its finescale rail for 'N' gauge. Standard 'N' gauge code 80 rail joiners can be used to join the track and points together from Peco with a choice of left and right medium radius Unifrog turnouts

plus yard lengths of flexible track and plastic buffer stops to assemble for the end of sidings. The Unifrog points can be wired for analogue or digital operation and critically (when fully wired) provide continuous power supply all the way through the point to prevent stalling of short wheelbase locomotives.

With these two track types already on the market the traditional choices of insulated frog and powered frogs are already available to 'TT:120' as well the option of finer rail profiles for those looking for greater realism.

However, the European market shouldn't be forgotten when it comes to track components, as 1:120 scale 'TT' modelling is already well »

Engineering samples allow Hornby's development team to assess the details and assemble of each new product for 'TT:120'.

Goods wagons are an important part of the product range including (from left) a 14ton tanker, a seven-plank open wagon and a GWR twin-vent 12ton box van.

Peco was the first to announce products for 'TT:120' in June 2022 including a collection of building kits and platform sections. This is its laser cut station building.

'TT:120' LAUNCHES

established in mainland Europe. One of the more popular 1:120 scale track ranges is that produces by Tillig, which offers two track systems: bedding track with a plastic ballast base for beginners together with its advanced track system which contains a range of track components suitable for building a wide range of layouts.

'TT:120' Accessories

No model railway is complete without its buildings and accessories and already there is a busy range of products both available now and on the way for release in 2023.

Alongside its track, Peco's June 2022 launch included kits for a station building, goods shed and signalbox using a combination of laser cut and plastic components that were joined by platform edges and surfacing for the growing 'TT:120' collection.

Hornby too saw the value of creating a complete system for 'TT:120', as it has with 'OO' gauge, with a new collection of Skaledale

Making progress is a 'TT:120' scale model of the Stanier 'Duchess'. This is a 3D printed sample to prove the CAD drawings.

Modern wagons in development include the BR HAA coal hopper as well as TTA tank wagons, Seacow ballast wagons and more.

The Gresley 'A3' will be released in LNER and BR era colour schemes. This decorated sample of 2550 *Blink Bonny* is due to receive adjustments to its livery application before production, including correction of the wheel colour.

buildings starting with a set of railway structures based on Dent station and set to grow in 2023 with items including a 1930s house, a church, a fuel station, terrace houses and more to allow realistic model railway.

Expanding the Hornby collection further is its connection with Oxford Diecast with the diecast vehicle manufacturer entering the 'TT:120' scale market with a collection of road vehicles to complement Hornby's new railway range. These will model the Bedford OB coach, Dennis F12 fire engine, Land Rover Series 2, Morris 1000, Austin taxi and Scammell Mechanical Horse.

At the 2022 Great Electric Train Show West Hill Wagon Works revealed it was joining the 'TT:120' race with an extensive collection of 3D printed accessories including GRC lineside cable trunking, fencing, buffer stops, depot accessories, 3D printed bogies, engines, a dumper truck, speed restriction signs, buckets, bins and much more.

'TT:120' Future
The birth of 'TT:120' for the British market has been rapid this year and this new scale looks set for a bright future as more companies offer products to expand the options available and the level of detail possible. Hornby's arrival in 'TT:120' will be a driving force in ready-to-run locomotives and rolling stock and we can't wait to get our hands on the first products. Keep watching Hornby Magazine and KeyModelWorld for the latest in 'TT:120' products and news.

• Visit *www.keymodelworld.com/tt120-model-railways* for more information. ∎

A full collection of HST power cars and trailer coaches are in development. The power cars are at the CAD phase with 3D printed proving samples produced, while the matching Mk 3 carriages have reached the engineering sample phase.

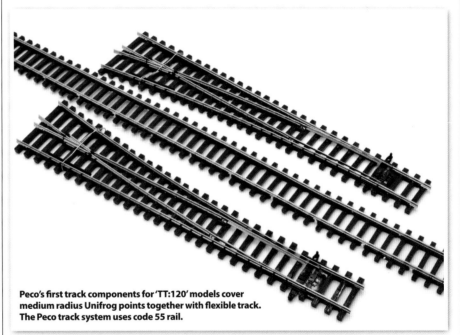

Peco's first track components for 'TT:120' models cover medium radius Unifrog points together with flexible track. The Peco track system uses code 55 rail.

Peco's new building kits for the scale use laser cut wood parts as well as plastic mouldings.

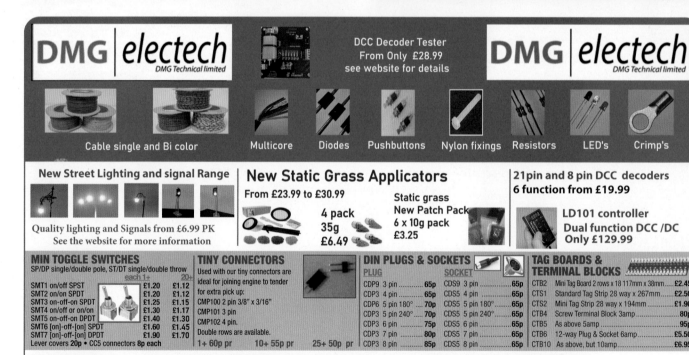

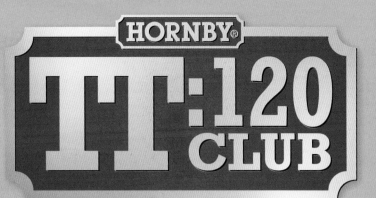

Join the Hornby TT:120 Club today!

Gain access to exclusive features, discounts, promotions and content.

LIMITED TIME OFFER* FREE Annual Membership

Exclusive 15%* DISCOUNT**

Annual Membership From £30**

Hornby TT:120 Club Membership benefits include:

Join before 01.02.23 for **FREE** annual Membership*

- Quarterly 36 page Club Magazine featuring tips, articles and guides
- TT:120 Membership card, pin badge and lanyard
- Advance notice of uncatalogued releases
- Free access to the Hornby Visitor Centre
- Half price Family Ticket (max. 4) to Hornby Visitor Centre
- Exclusive Club Members area on website
- Free access to the Hornby Members' Room at selected exhibitions
- Free competition entry into the Annual Best Hornby TT:120 layout (T&Cs applicable)
- Access to special bundle deals
- Monthly email updates
- Exclusive Club models

Scan the QR code to go directly to
www.hornby.com/HornbyTT120-club

* Sign up to the Hornby TT:120 Club by 31.1.23 for free membership.
From 1.2.23, the standard Membership Fee will apply:

** £30 UK Membership £35 Rest of the World (excluding Australia).

*** Discount will be automatically applied at basket for Hornby TT:120 Members only.
The discount will apply for the duration of the 12-month subscription.
Subject to availability. Prices as of December 2022.

For more information or to join The Hornby TT:120 Club
visit **www.hornby.com/HornbyTT120-club** or call **01843 233512**

 facebook.com /officialhornby   twitter.com /hornby   instagram.com /officialhornby   tiktok.com /officialhornby   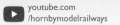 youtube.com /hornbymodelrailways   **Beyond the Buffers** HORNBY podcast   spotify.com Beyond the Buffers

Forward to 2023

Unique steam locomotives, historic diesels and the latest locos and rolling stock are all part of the big plans for ready-to-run. **MIKE WILD** surveys the extensive lists of new models currently in development for release in 2023 and beyond.

With more than 240 new models in development it is fair to say that the model railway hobby is thriving despite facing big challenges around pricing and shipping. 2022 has seen price rises come in from many model manufacturers, while the zero COVID policy in China has made the process of making models even more unpredictable than before due to immediate local lockdowns forcing factories to send their workforce home temporarily.

But despite all these problems we still have a huge number of new models to look forward to in 2023 and beyond as our manufacturers continue to create ever more innovative and, in some cases, exotic motive power and rolling stock.

2022 has also seen the arrival of another new scale for the British market – 'TT:120'. We haven't included the product listings for 'TT:120' in this survey, as they are included in full on pages 108-115, but it must be said that having seen the pre-production samples this new scale is already looking very attractive.

In this survey we are covering 'OO' gauge together with 'N', 'O', 'OO9' and 'O-16.5' to gather all planned new products you can expect in the locomotive and rolling stock department. Within the listing are more than 120 locos, with almost the same number of carriages and wagons in production too. And there is something for everyone from compact tank engines for industrial layouts through to the biggest main line locos to haul scale length express trains.

'OO' Gauge

New announcements keep coming for 'OO' gauge and even in the final weeks before this Yearbook closed for press, we saw KR Models reveal plans to model the unique Midland Railway-built Lickey Banker 0-10-0 'Big Bertha' and Locomotion Models announce a model of the North Eastern Railway ES1 electrics, while Accurascale and Revolution Trains both revealed new wagon projects at the 2022 Great Electric Train Show.

'OO' gauge is still the central focus of the British model railway market with an impressive 63 locos in development together with 55 carriage and wagon projects. While we still see traditional annual announcements from Hornby, Bachmann has moved to quarterly releases, which means that several of its 2022 products have already been delivered, including the

Rails of Sheffield and Dapol have partnered to create a 'OO' gauge ready-to-run model of the SECR 'D1' 4-4-0. A decorated sample of British Railways lettered 31487 leads a 'Birdcage' set on the Hornby Magazine test track. *Mike Wild*

Accurascale's Class 37s are approaching completion with delivery expected this winter. This is 97301 in Network Rail yellow. Accurascale

Double Fairlie 0-4-4-0T, Class 37 and in early November the Penrhyn Mainline Hunslet 0-4-0STs.

An interesting evolution in recent years has been the increased focus on unique locos. Currently we can expect a model of the LMS 'Turbomotive' steam turbine 'Pacific' from Hornby in 2023 together with KR Models' Bulleid 'Leader' 0-6-0+-0-6-0 and Rails of Sheffield's models of Metropolitan Vickers gas turbine prototype 18100 and its subsequent rebuilding as a prototype electric loco. Heljan is also working on a model of North British prototype Bo-Bo diesel 10800.

Industrial locomotives have also continued to find favour in 'OO' gauge with Dapol working on a Hawthorn Leslie 0-4-0ST, KR Models' a Hunslet Bo-Bo diesel and Rapido Trains UK the Hunslet 16in 0-6-0ST. Rapido Trains UK has also been proving to be prolific in announcing new loco and rolling stock projects for 'OO' gauge totalling 12 items. Its biggest is the long-requested Highland Railway 'Jones Goods' 4-6-0, while its rolling stock models have picked off missing links in the steam era goods world including SECR and GWR freight wagons.

The arrival of Accurascale's first powered model in 2022 – the Class 55 'Deltic' – has set the stage for its next releases that are set to be the Class 92 Co-Co dual voltage electric and Class 37 Co-Co diesel. These will be followed by the GWR 'Manor' 4-6-0 and then the Brush Class 31. And we can't move on without mentioning the Class 89 Co-Co electric, which is being made for 'OO' in a partnership between Accurascale and Rails of Sheffield.

Hornby has exciting new steam locomotives in progress including a tantalising collection of all-new Gresley 'P2' 2-8-2s for LNER period modellers, while the specification for its new LMS 'Black Five' 4-6-0 promises working lights, firebox flicker, a 21-pin decoder socket and a version with a factory fitted smoke generator. Modern modellers haven't been forgotten either as Hornby is working towards completion of its Stadler Class 755 'Flirt' bi-mode units. »

TABLE 1 – 'OO' GAUGE NEW LOCOMOTIVE PROJECTS 2023 FORWARDS			
Product	**Region**	**Manufacturer**	**Expected**
L&MR 0-4-2 Lion/Thunderbolt	Midland/Western	Rapido Trains UK	2023
Highland Railway 'Jones Goods' 4-6-0	Scottish	Rapido Trains UK	2023
GWR steam railmotor	Western	Kernow MRC	2023
GWR '43XX' 2-6-0 (new variants)	Western	Dapol	2023
GWR 'Manor' 4-6-0	Western	Accurascale	2023
GWR '15XX' 0-6-0PT	Western	Rapido Trains UK	2023
LBSCR 'E1' 0-6-0T	Southern	Rapido Trains UK	2023
SECR 'D1' 4-4-0	Southern	Rails/Dapol	2022
SR Bulleid 'Leader' 0-6-0+0-6-0	Southern	KR Models	2023
MR 'Big Bertha' 0-10-0 2290/58100	Midland	KR Models	TBA
LMS 'Black Five' 4-6-0	Midland	Hornby	2023
LMS 'Turbomotive' 4-6-2	Midland	Hornby	2023
GCR 'A5' 4-6-2T	Eastern	Sonic Models	2022
NER 'J26' 0-6-0	Eastern	Oxford Rail	2023
LNER 'A4' 4-6-2 (die-cast body)	Eastern	Hornby (Dublo)	2022
LNER 'G5' 0-4-4T	Eastern	TMC/Bachmann	2023
LNER 'P2' 2-8-2 (2002)	Eastern	Hornby	2023
LNER 'P2' 2-8-2 (2007)	Eastern	Hornby	2023
LNER 'P2' 2-8-2 (2003) (streamlined)	Eastern	Hornby	2023
LNER 'P2' 2-8-2 (2007/steam gen)	Eastern	Hornby	2023
BR '2MT' 2-6-0	Various	Hornby	2022
Hawthorn Leslie 0-4-0ST	Industrial	Dapol	2023
Haydock Foundry 0-6-0WT	Industrial	KR Models	2023
Hunslet 16in 0-6-0ST	Industrial	Rapido Trains UK	2022
GWR AEC parcels railcar	Western	Heljan	2023
DHP1 prototype Bo-Bo	Midland	KR Models	2023
Hunslet 1,124hp Bo-Bo diesel	Industrial	KR Models	2023
Met-Vic 18100 gas turbine	Western	Rails/Heljan	2023
Met-Vic E1000/E2001 25kV electric	Midland	Rails/Heljan	2023
NBL pioneer diesel-electric 10800	Various	Heljan	2023
Ruston & Hornsby 88DS 0-4-0	Various	Hornby	2022
Ruston & Hornsby 165DE 0-6-0	Various	Heljan	2023
NER ES1 Bo-Bo electric	Eastern	Locomotion/Rails/Heljan	2022
Class 02 0-4-0	Various	Heljan	2023
Class 04 Drewry 0-6-0 diesel shunter	Eastern/Southern	Rapido Trains UK	TBA
Class 18 Clayton CBD90 Bo-Bo	Industrial	Revolution Trains	2023
Class 25/1 Bo-Bo	Various	Bachmann	2023
Class 25/2 Bo-Bo	Various	Bachmann	2023
Class 25/2 and 25/3 Bo-Bos	Various	SLW	2023
Class 26 (new tooling) Bo-Bo	Scottish	Heljan	2023
Class 31 A1A-A1A	Various	Accurascale	2023
Class 33/2 (original condition) Bo-Bo	Southern	Heljan	2023
Class 37/0 Co-Co	Various	Accurascale	2022
Class 37/4 (modern era) Co-Co	Various	Accurascale	2022
Class 37/6 and 37/7 Co-Cos	Various	Accurascale	2022
Class 43 HST power cars	Various	Hornby	2022
Class 47 Co-Co	Various	Heljan	2023
Class 56 Co-Co	Midland/Eastern	Cavalex Models	2023
Class 59 Co-Co	Western/Eastern	Dapol	2022
Class 69 Co-Co	Various	Bachmann	TBA
Class 73/9 Bo-Bo electro-diesel	Scottish/Southern	KMS Railtech	TBC
Class 89 Co-Co electric	Eastern	Rails/Accurascale	2023
Class 92 Co-Co electric	Various	Accurascale	2022
Class 93 tri-mode Bo-Bo	Rail Ops Group	Revolution Trains	2023/2024
Class 97 (ex-Class 37) Co-Co	Various	Accurascale	2022
Class 104 two- and three-car DMU	Midland/Scotland	Heljan	2023
Class 142 two-car DMU	Midland/Eastern	Realtrack	2023
Class 175 two-car DMU	Midland/Wales	Revolution Trains	2023
Class 175 three-car DMU	Midland/Wales	Revolution Trains	2023
Class 180 five-car DMU	Various	Revolution Trains	2023
Class 755/3 three-car Bi-MU	Great Eastern	Hornby	2023
Class 755/4 four-car Bi-MU	Great Eastern	Hornby	2023
4-DD four-car EMU	Southern	KR Models	2023
Total: 63	**Steam: 24**	**Diesel/Electric: 39**	

2023 will also see Sonic Models deliver its first 'OO' gauge ready-to-run loco – in the shape of Robinson 'A5' 4-6-2T – which will be available exclusively through Rails of Sheffield. The same retailer is also working with Dapol on a new model of the SECR 'D1' 4-4-0s for 'OO'.

Heljan's place in the 'OO' gauge market has also been cemented in recent years with 2023 due to see it release its all-new Class 47 as well as the North British prototype 10800, the GWR AEC parcels railcar, the Yorkshire Engine Company Class 02 0-4-0 and potentially the Class 104 DMU too.

For the full list of 'OO' gauge ready-to-run projects see Table 1 and Table 2.

'O' Gauge

The popularity of 'O' gauge modelling has continued to grow with the main names in mass-produced ready-to-run being Dapol and Heljan. However, Rapido Trains UK has also dipped its toe in the water for 'O' gauge with a proposal for a model of the LNER 'J70' 0-6-0T, while Flangeway Models is working on a model of the ZZA snowplough an ZUA 'Mermaid' ballast tippler too.

Also firmly in the 'O' gauge market is Ellis Clark Trains. 2022 has been a busy year for the company which released its first home-grown ready-to-run model in the Presflo cement hopper that was followed soon after by its

latest collaboration with Darstaed Trains to produce the Thompson corridor stock. Ellis Clark is now working on an all-new collection of Pullman cars for 'O' gauge with Darstaed, while in the works for direct manufacturing are its Stanier 'Black Five' 4-6-0, Wickham Type 27 trolley and trailer, plus recently announced model of the 'Shark' ballast plough plus 'Seacow' and 'Sealion' ballast hoppers.

Dapol has continued to build its portfolio of smaller locos with the current projects including the LSWR 'B4' 0-4-0T and Hunslet 'Austerity'/LNER 'J94' 0-6-0ST for the scale, while its Lionheart Trains brand is developing a model of the BR '3MT' 2-6-2T next in 'O'. Dapol is also continuing work on its 'O' gauge Class 66. Rolling stock projects include new GWR and LMS pattern 12ton ventilated vans in 'O' for the steam era as well as the TTA tanker for diesel era layouts – a popular and much wanted model.

Heljan continues to focus on the diesel era market having placed its plans for the GWR '2251' 0-6-0 on hold in 2021. Currently it is working on 13 new diesel projects ranging in size from the compact Yorkshire Engine Co Class 02 0-4-0 through to the huge Class 45 'Peak' in later condition with sealed beam lights. The next releases will be the Class 26 and 27 BRCW Bo-Bo diesels that will be the first from Heljan to feature plug-and-play DCC interfaces using the ESU L decoder arrangement. They will also have increased

Bachmann's 'OO9' Quarry Hunslet 0-4-0STs are due for release in early 2023. Bachmann

functionality including cab lights and engine room lights setting the stall out for future releases.

Also on the cards currently are all-new versions of the Class 37/0 in split and centre headcode forms with cutaway buffer beams, a revised Class 55 'Deltic' to model the class in later life, the enticing Class 73 Bo-Bo electro-diesel plus its long-awaited collection of Pressed Steel and Gloucester DMUs, modelling the Class 117, 121 and 122 plus matching trailer cars for the single-car DMUs.

Not to be forgotten in ready-to-run 'O' gauge are the small production, high detail brass models produced by Lee Marsh Models, Masterpiece Models and 55H. These products are in a different league in presentation and pricing, but offer sought after super detailed ready-to-run steam locos, with current plans including a new model of the Gresley 'A3' 4-6-2, BR '5MT' 4-6-0, LBSCR 'Atlantics' and more.

See Tables 3 and 4 for the full list of 'O' gauge locomotive and rolling stock projects.

'N' Gauge

After a relatively quiet period, 'N' gauge has seen renewed interest with a spate of new product announcements from Dapol, Revolution Trains and Rapido Trains UK. There are two additional names working on 'N' gauge products – namely Graham Farish and Sonic Models.

Revolution Trains has the largest number of 'N' gauge projects to its name ranging from the Class 59 heavy-freight Co-Co diesels to the Swindon Cross-Country Class 120 DMUs, Class 128 parcels railcar and modern Class 377 Electrostar units. In addition, Revolution is also developing several rolling stock models of Pullman carriages, Cartic4 articulated car transporters, engineering stock and more.

Rapido Trains UK made the Class 28 Co-Bo its first »

The Highland Railway 'Jones Goods' is being developed for 'OO' gauge by Rapido Trains. Rapido Trains UK

Hornby's all-new model of the Gresley 'P2' 2-8-2 will recreate specific locomotives, including new build loco 2007 *Prince of Wales*. Hornby

TABLE 2 – 'OO' GAUGE NEW ROLLING STOCK PROJECTS 2023 FORWARDS			
Product	**Region**	**Manufacturer**	**Expected**
GWR/BR Siphon G	Western	Accurascale	2023
GWR Toplight 'City' non-corridor Brake Third	Western	Dapol	2022/2023
GWR Toplight 'City' non-corridor Third	Western	Dapol	2022/2023
GWR Toplight 'City' non-corridor Composite	Western	Dapol	2022/2023
SR GM Inspection Saloon/Caroline	Southern/Various	Revolution Trains	2023
LNER 'Coronation' Brake /Kitchen Third	LNER	Hornby	2023
LNER 'Coronation' Double Open First	LNER	Hornby	2023
LNER 'Coronation' Open/Kitchen Third	LNER	Hornby	2023
LNER 'Coronation' Open/Brake Third	LNER	Hornby	2023
LNER 'Coronation' Observation Car	LNER	Hornby	2023
BR Mk 1 57ft suburban Brake Second	Various	Accurascale	2023
BR Mk 1 57ft suburban Composite	Various	Accurascale	2023
BR Mk 1 57ft suburban Second Open	Various	Accurascale	2023
BR Mk 1 57ft suburban Composite Lavatory	Various	Accurascale	2023
BR Mk 1 57ft suburban Second Lavatory Open	Various	Accurascale	2023
BR Mk 1 57ft suburban Second	Various	Accurascale	2023
BR Mk 2b Brake Corridor First	Various	Accurascale	2023
BR Mk 2b Corridor First/Corridor Second	Various	Accurascale	2023
BR Mk 2b Tourist Second Open	Various	Accurascale	2023
Caledonian Sleeper Mk 5 carriages	Midland	Accurascale	2022
GWR Class 802/1 four-coach pack	Western	Hornby	2022
LNER Class 801/2 four-coach pack	Eastern	Hornby	2022
Trans-Pennine Mk 5 carriage sets	Midland/Eastern	Accurascale	2022
Ex-Wisbech and Upwell Tramcar	Film	Rapido Trains UK	2023
GWR Loriot Y	Western	Hornby	2022
GWR Loriot Y	Western	Rapido Trains UK	2022
GWR 'Toad' brake van	Western	Rapido Trains UK	2022
GWR 'Iron Mink' van	Western	Rapido Trains UK	2023
GWR O21 four-plank open wagon	Western	Rapido Trains UK	2023
GWR 'Siphon G' bogie van	Western	Accurascale	2023
SECR six-wheel brake van	Southern	Rapido Trains UK	2023
SR banana van (Dia. 1478)	Southern	Accurascale	2023
SR banana van (Dia. 1479)	Southern	Accurascale	2023
BR Borail B bogie wagon	Various	Revolution Trains	2022
BR Borail C bogie wagon	Various	Revolution Trains	2022
BR 'Mullet' bogie wagon	Various	Revolution Trains	2022
BR YQA 'Parr' bogie wagon	Various	Revolution Trains	2022
BR YQA 'Super Tench' wagon	Various	Revolution Trains	2022
BR Cartic-4 car carriers	Various	Revolution Trains	2023
BR Palbrick B brick wagon	Various	KR Models	2023
BIA/BWA/BXA/BZA covered steel carrier	Various	Cavalex Models	TBC
CDA china clay hopper	Various	KMS/Trains 4U/ Cavalex	2022
Cowans Sheldon 15ton crane	Various	Oxford Rail	TBC
FNA-D Nuclear flask carrier	Various	Revolution Trains	2023
FNA-D Nuclear flask carrier	Various	Accurascale	2023
FWA Ecofret container flats	Various	Revolution Trains	2022
IPA car carriers	Various	Revolution Trains	2022
HOA hopper wagon	Various	Revolution Trains	2022
JGA/PHA bogie aggregate wagon	Various	Cavalex Models	2023
KSA Rover Cube wagons	Various	Revolution Trains	TBA
KSA timber carriers	Various	Revolution Trains	TBA
OAA open wagon	Various	Rapdio Trains UK	2023
PHA/JYA bogie aggregate box wagons	Western	Cavalex Models	2023
TUA caustic soda tank	Various	Revolution/Rainbow Railways	2023
Torpedo ore wagon	Industrial	KR Models	2023
VIX Ferry van	Various	Rapido Trains UK	2023
Total: 55			

Locomotion Models, Rails of Sheffield and Heljan are creating an exclusive model of the North Eastern Railway Bo-Bo electric ES1 for 'OO' gauge. *Richard Watson*

TABLE 3 – 'O' GAUGE NEW LOCOMOTIVE PROJECTS 2023 FORWARDS			
Product	**Region**	**Manufacturer**	**Expected**
GWR '850' 0-6-0ST	Western	Lee Marsh Models	2022
GWR 'Castle' 4-6-0	Western	Lee Marsh Models	TBC
GNR 'C1' 4-4-2	Eastern	Masterpiece Models	TBC
GNR 'C2' 4-4-2	Eastern	Masterpiece Models	TBC
LBSCR 'H1' 4-4-2	Southern	Masterpiece Models	TBC
LBSCR 'H2' 4-4-2	Southern	Masterpiece Models	TBC
LSWR 'B4' 0-4-0T	Southern	Dapol	2023
LMS 'Black Five' 4-6-0	Midland	Ellis Clark/Darstaed	2023
LMS rebuilt 'Royal Scot' 4-6-0	Midland	Masterpiece Models	TBC
LMS rebuilt 'Patriot' 4-6-0	Midland	Masterpiece Models	TBC
LNER 'A1'/'A3' 4-6-2	Eastern	Masterpiece Models	Proposed
LNER 'A1'/'A3' 4-6-2	Eastern	Lee Marsh Models	2023
LNER 'J70' 0-6-0T	Eastern	Rapido Trains UK	TBA
LNER 'J94' 0-6-0ST	Eastern/Industrial	Dapol	2023
BR '5MT' 4-6-0	Various	55H	2023
BR '5MT' 4-6-0	Various	Masterpiece Models	TBC
BR '4MT' 4-6-0	Various	55H	2023
BR '4MT' 2-6-0	Various	55H	2023
BR '4MT' 2-6-4T	Various	Lee Marsh Models	2023
BR '3MT' 2-6-2T	Various	Lionheart Trains	2023
Class 02 0-4-0 shunter	Various	Heljan	2023
Class 09 0-6-0 shunter	Southern	Gaugemaster/Dapol	TBA
Class 26 Bo-Bo	Eastern/Scottish	Heljan	2022
Class 27 Bo-Bo	Midland/Scottish	Heljan	2022
Class 37/0 (split headcodes) Co-Co	Various	Heljan	2023
Class 37/0 (centre headcodes) Co-Co	Various	Heljan	2023
Class 45 1Co-Co1 (sealed beam headlights)	Midland/Eastern	Heljan	2023
Class 55 Co-Co (revised tooling)	Eastern	Heljan	2023
Class 66 Co-Co	All	Dapol	2023
Class 73/1 Bo-Bo electro-diesel	Southern	Heljan	2023
Class 117 three-car DMU	Western/Midland	Heljan	2023
Class 121 single-car DMU	Western/Midland	Heljan	2023
Class 122 single-car DMU	Western/Midland	Heljan	2023
Class 149 trailer car	Western/Midland	Heljan	2023
Class 150 trailer car	Western/Midland	Heljan	2023
GWR streamlined railcar	Western	Dapol	2022
Wickham Trolley and trailers	Various	Ellis Clark Trains	2023
Total: 37	**Steam:** 20	**Diesel:** 17	

The Class 31 A1A-A1A diesel-electrics are one of the most recent project announcements from Accurascale. One of the first engineering samples takes a turn on the *Hornby Magazine* test track. Mike Wild

The Class 90 Bo-Bo AC electric is getting a fresh new model in 'N' gauge from **Graham Farish.** Bachmann

Above: **Hornby's 2022 plans include models of the Stadler Class 755 'Flirt' units for 'OO' gauge. This is the latest CAD drawing for the new model.** Hornby

The LMS 'Turbomotive' from Hornby's 2022 range is making rapid progress towards production for 'OO'. Hornby

The unique Class 89 is being offered for 'OO' gauge by Accurascale and Rails of Sheffield. The first samples are expected before the end of 2022. Accurascale

announcement for the scale in 2021 and this model has now advanced to the decorated samples stage, while Rapido has also revealed that is working on a new model of the Class 44 1Co-Co1 original 'Peak' series diesels, with plans to continue with all-new models of the Class 45 and 46 for the scale in the future too.

Graham Farish isn't quite so busy on the 'N' gauge front, but its three outstanding loco projects have been joined by an exciting and often requested Class 90 AC electric. This all-new model is set to leave the previous Poole-made Class 90 in the shade by offering extensive detail options, NEM coupling pockets, a new mechanism, DCC controllable lights, a factory fitted speaker and more. It joins the Class 69 Co-Co diesel, Class 158 DMU and Class 450 EMU in the Graham Farish 'N' gauge project list.

Meanwhile Dapol is working through five 'N' gauge loco projects covering the GWR '63XX' 2-6-0, a full refresh of its Drummond 'M7' 0-4-4T, all-new 'West Country'

4-6-2s plus the Class 59 diesel, and it also has the O&K JHA stone hoppers in development for 'N' to go with the Class 59.

Last, but by no means least, is Sonic Models, which is currently working on two loco projects: the GWR 'Large Prairie' 2-6-2T and the LNER 'J50' 0-6-0T. Both are significantly advanced with engineering samples completed ahead of expected release in 2023.

See Tables 5 and 6 for the full list of 'N' gauge locomotive and rolling stock projects.

Narrow gauge

Completing our survey of new products is the growth of ready-to-run narrow gauge models in both 'OO9' (4mm:1ft scale models running on 9mm gauge track) and 'O-16.5' (7mm:1ft scale models running on 16.5mm gauge track).

'OO9' is the most advanced and since our last survey Bachmann has introduced two enticing narrow gauge steam locos to the market – the Ffestiniog Double Fairlie 0-4-4-0T and, by the time this Yearbook reaches the shops, its November announcement of the Penrhyn Mainline Hunslet 0-4-0ST should also be in stock (see full review in HM187).

These two models have come through between our surveys, but Bachmann is still beavering away on its models of the smaller Quarry Hunslet 0-4-0ST as well as ≫

TABLE 4 – 'O' GAUGE NEW ROLLING STOCK PROJECTS 2023 FORWARDS			
Vehicle	Region	Manufacturer	Expected
GWR Siphon G bogie van	Western	Minerva Models	2023
GWR N32 'Felix Pole' coal wagon	Western	Minerva Models	2023
LBSCR Stroudley four-wheel Brake Third	Southern	Dapol	2023
LBSCR Stroudley four-wheel Third	Southern	Dapol	2023
LBSCR Stroudley four-wheel Second	Southern	Dapol	2023
LBSCR Stroudley four-wheel First	Southern	Dapol	2023
LBSCR Stroudley four-wheel Composite	Southern	Dapol	2023
LMS 50ft Inspection Saloon	Various	Heljan	2023
Pullman K Type Brake Parlour Third	Various	Ellis Clark/Darstaed	2023
Pullman K Type Parlour First	Various	Ellis Clark/Darstaed	2023
Pullman K Type Parlour Third	Various	Ellis Clark/Darstaed	2023
Pullman K Type Kitchen First	Various	Ellis Clark/Darstaed	2023
Pullman K Type Kitchen Third	Various	Ellis Clark/Darstaed	2023
BR Mk 2 FK	All	Heljan	2023
BR Mk 2 TSO	All	Heljan	2023
BR Mk 2 BSO	All	Heljan	2023
BR Mk 2 BFK	All	Heljan	2023
SR CCT/PMV four-wheel parcels van	Various	Heljan	2023
GWR 'Toad' brake van	Western	Dapol	2023
GWR MOGO 12ton box van	Western	Dapol	2023
GWR 12ton box van	Western	Dapol	2022
GWR Fruit Van A	Western	Dapol	2022
LMS 12ton box van	Midland	Dapol	2022
HAA MGR covered hopper	Midland/Eastern	Dapol	2022
TTA 45ton tank wagon	Various	Dapol	TBA
YGB 'Sealion' ballast hopper	Various	Ellis Clark Trains	2023
YGB 'Seacow' ballast hopper	Various	Ellis Clark Trains	2023
ZJV 'Mermaid' ballast tippler	Various	Flangeway/Dapol	TBA
ZUA 'Shark' ballast plough	Various	Ellis Clark Trains	2023
ZZA snowplough	Various	Flangeway/Dapol	TBA
Total: 28			

TABLE 5 – 'N' GAUGE NEW LOCOMOTIVE PROJECTS 2023 FORWARDS			
Vehicle	Region	Manufacturer	Expected
GWR 'Large Prairie' 2-6-2T	Western	Sonic Models	2023
GWR '63XX' 2-6-0	Western	Dapol	TBA
LSWR 'M7' 0-4-4T	Southern	Dapol	2023
SR air-smoothed 'West Country' 4-6-2	Southern	Dapol	TBA
SR rebuilt 'West Country' 4-6-2	Southern	Dapol	TBA
LNER 'J50' 0-6-0T	Eastern	Sonic Models	2023
Class 28 Co-Bo	Midland	Rapido Trains UK	2023
Class 44 1Co-Co1	Midland	Rapido Trains UK	2023
Class 45 1Co-Co1	Midland/Eastern	Rapido Trains UK	TBA
Class 46 1Co-Co1	Various	Rapido Trains UK	TBA
Class 59 Co-Co diesel	Western/Eastern	Dapol	2023
Class 59 Co-Co diesel	Western/Eastern	Revolution Trains	2023
Class 69 Co-Co diesel	Various	Graham Farish	TBA
Class 90 Bo-Bo electric	Midland/Eastern	Graham Farish	
Class 120 Swindon cross-country DMU	Western	Revolution Trains	TBA
Class 128 Parcels railcar	Western/Midland	Revolution Trains	2023
Class 158 two-car DMU	Various	Graham Farish	2023
Class 175 two-car DMU	Midlands/Wales	Revolution Trains	2023
Class 175 three-car DMU	Midlands/Wales	Revolution Trains	2023
Class 180 five-car DMU	Various	Revolution Trains	2023
Class 313/314 EMU	Various	Revolution Trains	2023
Class 377 Electrostar EMU	Western/Southern	Revolution Trains	TBA
Class 450 EMU	Southern	Graham Farish	2023
LT 1938 tube stock	London	Revolution Trains	2023
Total: 24	**Steam: 6**	**Diesel/Electric: 18**	

TABLE 6 – 'N' GAUGE NEW ROLLING STOCK PROJECTS 2023 FORWARDS			
Vehicle	Region	Manufacturer	Expected
SR GM Inspection Saloon/Caroline	Southern	Revolution Trains	2023
Pullman K Type all-steel Brake Parlour Third	Various	Revolution Trains	2023
Pullman K Type all-steel Parlour First	Various	Revolution Trains	2023
Pullman K Type all-steel Parlour Third	Various	Revolution Trains	2023
Pullman K Type all-steel Kitchen First	Various	Revolution Trains	2023
Pullman K Type all-steel Kitchen Third	Various	Revolution Trains	2023
Trans Pennine Mk 5 carriage sets	Midland/Eastern	Revolution Trains	2022
Caledonian Sleeper Mk 5 carriages	Midland	Revolution Trains	2022
BR 24.5ton iron ore hoppers	Midland/Eastern	Revolution Trains	TBA
BR Borail B bogie wagon	Various	Revolution Trains	2023
BR Borail C bogie wagon	Various	Revolution Trains	2023
BR 'Mullet' bogie wagon	Various	Revolution Trains	2023
BR YQA 'Parr' bogie wagon	Various	Revolution Trains	2023
BR YQA 'Super Tench' wagon	Various	Revolution Trains	2023
BR Condor P container wagon	Midland/Scottish	Rapido Trains UK	2023
Cartic-4 car carriers	Various	Revolution Trains	2023
Class A 35ton tanker	Various	Revolution Trains	2023
FNA-D Nuclear flask carrier	Various	Revolution Trains	2023
FSA/FTA Freightliner container flats	Various	C=Rail	2023
IIA biomass bogie hoppers (Drax)	Eastern	Revolution Trains	2022
JIA NACCO china clay hopper	Western	EFE Rail	2022
MTV/ZKV Zander open wagon	Various	Revolution Trains	2022
O&K 102ton JHA hopper wagons	Western	Dapol	2022
PFA coal container flat wagons	Various	Revolution Trains	2022
PGA hopper wagons	Various	Cavalex/Rails	2022
PTA/JTA bogie tippler wagons	Various	Revolution Trains	TBA
VIX Ferry van	Various	N Gauge Society	TBA
Total: 27			

the Baguley-Drewry 4wDM shunter for 'OO9', which will be joined by a selection of Royal Army Naval Depot wagons.

Peco is also continuing to develop 'OO9' gauge products including Ffestiniog theme coaching stock; we are expecting to see more new product announcements from Peco following arrival of the Ffestiniog Quarryman's coaches in autumn 2022.

At the moment there is just one manufacturer working in 'O-16.5' scale for the British market, but this scale is well supported by kits for rolling stock, while there is also track available from Peco and typical buildings, road vehicles, figures and lineside equipment can be taken from 7mm scale product ranges. Dapol's Lionheart Trains brand is the first to step into this scale by developing models of the Lynton and Barnstaple Railway Manning Wardle 2-6-2Ts as well as

matching bogie coaches that are due to be delivered in 2023.

See Table 7 and Table 8 for the full list of 'OO9' and 'O-16.5' gauge model projects.

The future

Ready-to-run model production shows no signs of slowing down, despite the challenges that are being presented to

our hobby. Visits to events in 2022 has shown huge appetite for new models and across the scales too.

2023 and beyond are set to be very exciting times, with even more names making model railway locos and rolling stock than ever before and on a wide range of projects to suit almost every interest from pioneering railways to the present day and across the scales as well.

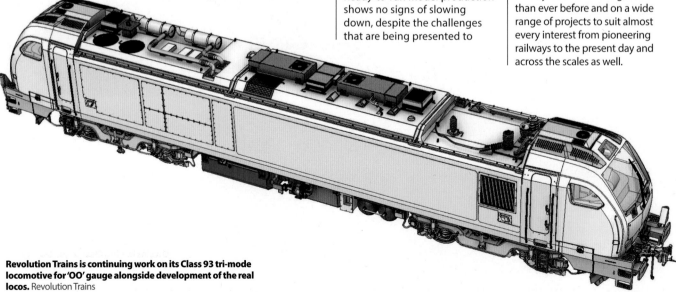

Revolution Trains is continuing work on its Class 93 tri-mode locomotive for 'OO' gauge alongside development of the real locos. Revolution Trains

TABLE 7 – 'OO9' GAUGE NEW PROJECTS 2023 FORWARDS			
Vehicle	**Region**	**Manufacturer**	**Expected**
Quarry Hunslet 0-4-0ST	Industrial	Bachmann	2023
Baguley-Drewry 4wDM	Industrial	Bachmann	TBA
Double Fairlie 0-4-4-0T	Ffestiniog	Peco/Kato	TBC
Ashover Light Railway carriage	Narrow gauge	Bachmann	TBA
FR 'Bowsider' coach	Ffestiniog	Peco	2023
RNAD open wagon	Narrow gauge	Bachmann	2023
RNAD flat wagon	Narrow gauge	Bachmann	2023
RNAD box van	Narrow gauge	Bachmann	2023
RNAD brake van	Narrow gauge	Bachmann	2023
Total: 9			

TABLE 8 – 'O-16.5' GAUGE NEW PROJECTS 2023 FORWARDS			
Vehicle	**Region**	**Manufacturer**	**Expected**
L&B Manning Wardle 2-6-2T	Southern	Lionheart Trains	2023
L&B bogie open third coach	Southern	Lionheart Trains	2023
L&B bogie compartment third	Southern	Lionheart Trains	2023
L&B bogie brake third	Southern	Lionheart Trains	2023
L&B bogie brake composite	Southern	Lionheart Trains	2023
Total: 5			

Keep watching in *Hornby Magazine* and at *www.keymodelworld.com* for the latest product announcements. The Warley National Model Railway Exhibition was just around the corner as this Yearbook closed for press and the Hornby January 2023 range launch wasn't far away either. We can't wait to see what is coming next. ∎

Heljan has received decorated samples of its model of NBL prototype 10800 for 'OO'. Heljan

Cavalex Models Class 56 for 'OO' has now reached the engineering sample stage. Cavalex Models

SELL YOUR MODELS

Scan me with your phone camera

THE PROCESS

1 Send us a list of your pre-owned items

LIST

2 We'll work with you to accurately value your collection

QUOTE

3 Either post your models to us or we can collect them from you

RECEIVE

4 Prompt payment made via your preferred method after items checked

PAYMENT

Why not exchange for a credit to spend in store or online for an even bigger payout!